Continue your adventure in history with three FREE historical novels from James Rada, Jr.

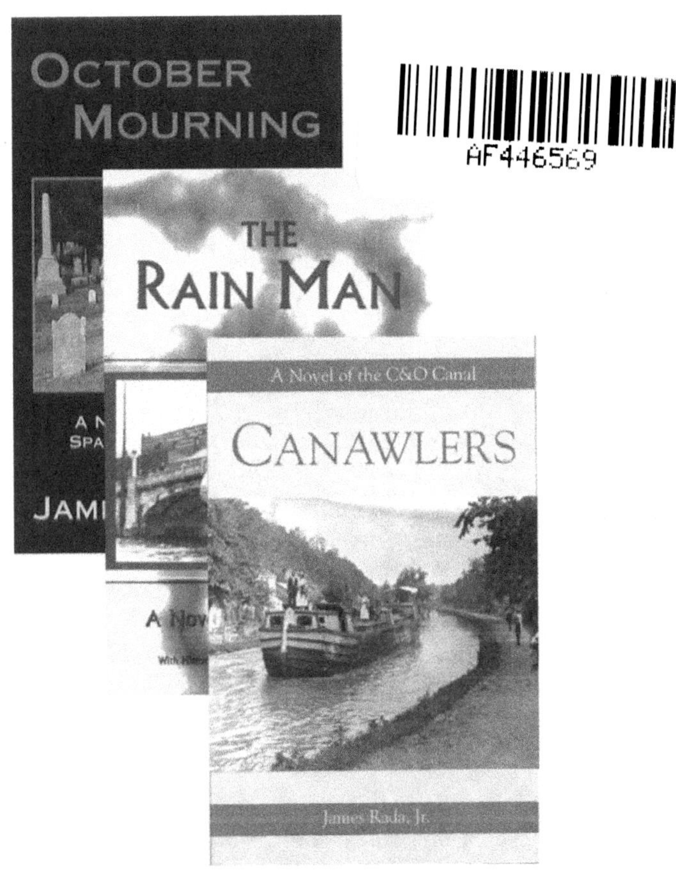

Visit *jamesrada.com/newsletter-email*
and enter your email
to receive your FREE novels.

CRITICAL ACCLAIM FOR
THE WORKS OF JAMES RADA, JR.

The Last to Fall

"Authors Jim Rada and Richard Fulton have done an outstanding job of researching and chronicling this little-known story of those Marines in 1922, marking it as a significant moment in Marine Corps history."

- GySgt. Thomas Williams
Executive Director
U.S. Marine Corps Historical Company

"Original, unique, profusely illustrated throughout, exceptionally well researched, informed, informative, and a bit iconoclastic, "The Last to Fall: The 1922 March, Battles, & Deaths of U.S. Marines at Gettysburg" will prove to be of enormous interest to military buffs and historians."

- Small Press Bookwatch

Saving Shallmar

"But Saving Shallmar's Christmas story is a tale of compassion and charity, and the will to help fellow human beings not only survive, but also be ready to spring into action when a new opportunity presents itself. Bittersweet yet heartwarming, Saving Shallmar is a wonderful Christmas season story for readers of all ages and backgrounds, highly recommended."

- Small Press Bookwatch

Battlefield Angels

"Rada describes women religious who selflessly performed life-saving work in often miserable conditions and thereby gained the admiration and respect of countless contemporaries. In so doing, Rada offers an appealing narrative and an entry point into the wealth of sources kept by the sisters."

- Catholic News Service

Between Rail and River

"The book is an enjoyable, clean family read, with characters young and old for a broad-based appeal to both teens and adults. Between Rail and River also provides a unique, regional appeal, as it teaches about a particular group of people, ordinary working 'canawlers' in a story that goes beyond the usual coverage of life during the Civil War."

- *Historical Fiction Review*

Canawlers

"A powerful, thoughtful and fascinating historical novel, Canawlers documents author James Rada, Jr. as a writer of considerable and deftly expressed storytelling talent."

- *Midwest Book Review*

"James Rada, of Cumberland, has written a historical novel for high-schoolers and adults, which relates the adventures, hardships and ultimate tragedy of a family of boaters on the C&O Canal. ... The tale moves quickly and should hold the attention of readers looking for an imaginative adventure set on the canal at a critical time in history."

- *Along the Towpath*

October Mourning

"This is a very good, and very easy to read, novel about a famous, yet unknown, bit of 20th Century American history. While reading this book, in your mind, replace all mentions of 'Spanish Flu' with 'bird flu.' Hmmm."

- *Reviewer's Bookwatch*

Secrets of the Western Maryland Railway

Little-Known Stories & Hidden History
About "Wild Mary"

Other non-fiction books by James Rada, Jr.

Non-Fiction

- Battlefield Angels: The Daughters of Charity Work as Civil War Nurses
- Beyond the Battlefield: Stories from Gettysburg's Rich History
- Clay Soldiers: One Marine's Story of War, Art, & Atomic Energy
- Echoes of War Drums: The Civil War in Mountain Maryland
- How to Make a Living Freelance Writing
- The Last to Fall: The 1922 March, Battles & Deaths of U.S. Marines at Gettysburg
- Looking Back: True Stories of Mountain Maryland
- Looking Back II: More True Stories of Mountain Maryland
- No North, No South: The Grand Reunion at the 50th Anniversary of the Battle of Gettysburg
- Saving Shallmar: Christmas Spirit in a Coal Town

Secrets Series

- Secrets of Allegany County: Little-Known Stories & Hidden History From Mountain Maryland
- Secrets of Catoctin Mountain: Little-Known Stories & Hidden History Along Catoctin Mountain
- Secrets of Deep Creek Lake: Little-Known Stories & Hidden History In and Around Maryland's Largest Lake
- Secrets of Franklin County: Little-Known Stories & Hidden History on Pennsylvania's State Line
- Secrets of Frederick County: Little-Known Stories & Hidden History About Maryland's Largest County
- Secrets of Garrett County: Little-Known Stories & Hidden History of Maryland's Westernmost County
- Secrets of the C&O Canal: Little-Known Stories & Hidden History Along the Potomac River
- Secrets of the Gettysburg Battlefield: Little-Known Stories & Hidden History from the Gettysburg Battlefield
- Secrets of the Washington County: Little-Known Stories & Hidden History Where Western Maryland Starts

For historical fiction by James Rada, Jr., visit jamesrada.com.

SECRETS OF THE WESTERN MARYLAND RAILWAY

Little-Known Stories & Hidden History About "Wild Mary"

by

James Rada, Jr.

LEGACY

PUBLISHING

A division of AIM Publishing Group

LEGACY

PUBLISHING

315 Oak Lane • Gettysburg, Pennsylvania 17325

CONTENTS

The Western Maryland Railway

Baltimore, Md., is well known as the starting point for the first steam-operated railroad in the country and the oldest U.S. railroad, the Baltimore and Ohio (B&O) Railroad. However, the city was also the starting point for another classic American railroad fourteen years later, the Western Maryland Railroad.

Unlike its larger brother, which operated in twelve states and Washington, D.C., the Western Maryland Railroad operated in only three; Maryland, Pennsylvania, and West Virginia.

The original railroad was chartered as the Baltimore, Carroll and Frederick Railroad in 1852. From Baltimore, the railroad moved west toward Washington County, Md. The following year, the Maryland General Assembly changed the name of the company to the Western Maryland Rail Road Company.

Once in Washington County, the railroad added a stop at Hagerstown, Md., and then Williamsport, Md. In Williamsport, it could take on coal from the Chesapeake and Ohio Canal and transport it to Baltimore. While the railroad began as a passenger operation, it eventually found its primary work in hauling coal, although passenger service did continue until 1958.

The railroad also built an extension into Pennsylvania, reaching Waynesboro and Shippensburg. A second line into Pennsylvania came about when the Western Maryland Railroad took over the Baltimore and Hanover Railroad and the Gettysburg Railroad.

This led to the Western Maryland Railroad becoming the

railroad that brought Abraham Lincoln to Gettysburg to deliver the Gettysburg Address. This, however, happened before the Western Maryland Railroad took control of the Gettysburg Railroad.

The Western Maryland Railroad hadn't fully lived up to its name by making its way into the heart of Western Maryland in its early decades. This didn't happen until the early 1900s when the C&O Canal allowed the railroad to use its rights of way and make its way to Cumberland, Md., where the Baltimore and Ohio Railroad had reached in 1842.

The Western Maryland Railroad, which changed its name to the Western Maryland Railway, passed quickly through West Virginia along this route, but it did not have any stops until it neared Cumberland. From Cumberland, the railroad moved southwest to Keyser, W.Va. It also moved through the coal towns of Georges Creek to Piedmont, W.Va. From there, it took over other railroad lines to move further into West Virginia. Its furthest stop west was in Webster Springs in central West Virginia.

The Chessie System took over the Western Maryland Railway in 1973. Then in 1975, many of the Western Maryland Railway lines were abandoned because they were parallel, and thus, redundant with Baltimore and Ohio Railroad lines.

The Western Maryland Railway was fully merged with the B&O in 1983, which then merged with the Chesapeake and Ohio Railway in 1987 and then, following a merger with the Seaboard System, it became CSX Transportation.

Today, a ghost of the old Western Maryland Railroad remains in the form of the Western Maryland Scenic Railroad that runs from Cumberland to Frostburg, Md. The Durbin & Greenbrier Valley Railroad, the Maryland Midland Railway, the Pennsylvania & Southern Railway and the York Railway also operate on lines that were part of the Western

Maryland Railroad.

A portion of the Baltimore Metro Subway uses the old roadbed of the Western Maryland Railroad going from Baltimore to Owings Mills, Md. Similarly, some of the roadbed is now rail trails, including the Western Maryland Rail Trail in Maryland, the Blackwater Canyon Trail and Allegheny Highlands Trail in West Virginia, and the Great Allegheny Passage in Maryland and Pennsylvania.

The Western Maryland Railway logo. Courtesy of Wikimedia Commons.

BUILDING A RAILROAD

I've Been Workin' on the Railroad

When the Western Maryland Railway built an extension line to Cumberland, Md., in 1903, it put the Baltimore and Ohio Railroad in an unwinnable position.

The Western Maryland Railway needed permission from the B&O Railroad to cross the Chesapeake and Ohio Canal since the B&O Railroad was running the canal by that time.

The storm that caused the Great Johnstown Flood had also forced the C&O Canal into receivership, and because the B&O Railroad held a great number of canal bonds, the railroad directors chose the receivers. So, essentially, the railroad was running the canal, not to make a profit, but to keep the Western Maryland Railway from reaching into Western Maryland.

To do that, the receivers had to keep the canal operating profitably. In December 1894, the B&O Railroad created the Chesapeake and Ohio Transportation Company of Washington County. According to the *Cumberland Evening Times*,

According to the *Cumberland Evening Times*, "The purposes of the corporation were to buy and lease lands, buy and transport timber, grain, fruits, seeds, &c., build boats and ships, mine coal, iron and other metals, open marble and slate quarries, operate canal boats by means of electricity, navigate the ocean by vessels, acquire bridges, wharves, &c., by lease or otherwise, and for other purposes." Its actual purpose appears to have been to create the illusion that the canal was operating at a profit so that it would remain open.

The choice the B&O Railroad directors were faced with in 1903 was to allow the Western Maryland Railway to cross the canal and start to lose trade to the railroad competitor or to pump money into the C&O Canal, which was costing the B&O Railroad money to make it look like the canal was turning a profit.

Workers building the Western Maryland Railroad along the C&O Canal pose in front of a crane. Picture is from the author's collection.

Either choice ultimately hurt the B&O Railroad. The directors made the choice they hoped would cause the least damage to the railroad.

The 60-mile Western Maryland Railway extension line began in Big Pool and moved west toward Cumberland.

"Though the route lay entirely in the Potomac River Valley, the going was far from easy, since the Baltimore and

Ohio Railroad, the Chesapeake and Ohio Canal and the National Turnpike had already been built on the best routes. Thus, Western Maryland needed 23 bridges to cross the Potomac River, five streams, the C&O Canal, the B&O Railroad and three county roads," Roger Cook and Karl Zimmerman wrote in *The Western Maryland Railway.*

Workers seemed to watching men with heavy equipment in the distance while building the Western Maryland Railroad west of Oldtown, Md. Sideling Hill can be seen in the distance. Picture is from the author's collection.

For the most part, the railroad route followed the path of the canal except in the area of the Paw Paw Bends. The railroad crossed back and forth over the Potomac River, while the canal went through the 3,118-foot-long Paw Paw Tunnel, the National Park Service calls "the greatest single engineering achievement on the canal." It is 22 feet wide and 24 feet wide and sheathed in more than 11 million bricks.

Vertical view of some of the heavy equipment used to build the Western Railroad in Allegany County, Md. Photo is from the author's collection.

"Linking those two points involved crossing the canal at various points, a privilege not readily obtained from receivers of the canal controlled by the B&O Railroad. With the help of the Maryland Legislature, rights were obtained, and payment for abutments, such as one at this point, helped the B&O recoup a little of its losses–the very losses it was incurring to keep the canal operating so that its rival, the Western Maryland Rail Road, might not acquire the route in a forced sale," Thomas Hahn wrote in his book, *Towpath Guide to the C&O Canal.*

Some of the workers who helped build the Western Maryland Railroad through Allegany County, Md. Photo is from the author's collection.

J. Q. Barlow was the chief engineer of the operation that required retaining walls be built on the canal to support the railroad bed. The extension was completed in 1906 and opened on March 15.

When the Western Maryland Railway opened its service in Cumberland, it became the fifth railroad (the others were Baltimore and Ohio Railroad, George's Creek and Cumberland Railroad, Cumberland and Pennsylvania Railroad, and the Cumberland and Westernport Electric Interurban Railway) to service the city. This is another reason that the B&O Railroad directors had decided that it was futile to continue holding off the Western Maryland Railway. In all, railroads employed 2,000 working in Cumberland, or roughly 10 percent of the population at the time.

More of the workers who helped build the Western Maryland Railroad through Allegany County, Md. Photo is from the author's collection.

The Western Maryland Railway continued to service Allegany County until the Chessie System absorbed it in the mid-1970s. Eventually, Chessie and the B&O would make up what would later be known as CSX.

The pictures illustrating this chapter were made from glass-plate negatives obtained at an estate auction. Research on the pictures at the Chesapeake and Ohio Canal Headquarters in Hagerstown led to the identification through poor-quality prints supplied by Thomas Hahn that these construction shots of the Western Maryland Railway were west of Sideling Hill near Oldtown. The most-likely location is the crossing at mile 159.5.

The track seen in this photo is narrow work track used by the workers to bring heavy equipment into and out of the area as they prepared the ground for the actual railroad track. Photo is from the author's collection.

The author has the original glass plates, and his collection has one more plate than the National Park Service collection. It is the first picture with this article.

You can see clothing styles, tools, heavy equipment and working conditions of the workers.

Glass-plate photography began around 1850 and was used up until around 1920. The process used to capture these images would have been the gelatin process introduced about 1880. The process used gelatin to disperse light-sensitive silver salts across the glass plate. The plates were then dried and stored away from the light until needed for use. These pictures of the construction of the railroad over the canal allow a glimpse into the working man's life at the beginning of the 20th century.

Another view showing the work track used by Western Maryland Railroad workers building track through Allegany County, Md. Photo is from the author's collection.

The Day Paw Paw
Almost Blew Up

It was a pleasant day in late April 1904 in Paw Paw, W.Va., when all of the bells and steams whistles in town began sounding.

"Look out! Look out! It's going off!" was the cry carried throughout the town.

For three days, residents of Paw Paw and the southeast corner of Allegany County, Md., had been watching cans of black powder carried into a shaft cut into the mountain next to the town. The final count was that 325 cans of powder weighing 8,125 pounds had been placed in the mountain and then the shaft was closed.

"As the number of cans disappearing in the mountain side increased the alarm of the people grew, and some in terror left the town, while those remaining filled their ears with cotton and waited for—they knew not what," the *Cumberland Evening Times* reported.

They had good reason to fear. When a similar cut had been made through Sideling Hill in Maryland, 1,400 cans of powder had been used. The resulting explosion threw rocks as heavy as half a ton hundreds of yards from the explosion site. Telegraph poles along the Baltimore and Ohio Railroad had been sheared off near the ground by flying debris.

The Fuller Syndicate, a group of wealthy financiers who were invested in railroads, had acquired the Western Maryland Railroad and West Virginia Central and Pittsburg Railway in 1902. Another railroad that the Fuller Syndicate owned was the Wabash Railroad. If the Western Maryland Railway could connect to the Wabash Railroad, the Fuller

Syndicate might be able to create a coast-to-coast railroad.

The following year an extension of the Western Maryland Railroad, which was renamed the Western Maryland Railway since it was under new ownership, was started to take the railroad into Western Maryland in direct competition with the B&O Railroad.

"Until the advent of the Wabash it was supposed there was no feasible route through the narrow gaps in the mountains between Cumberland and Hancock, forty miles, save those followed by the Chesapeake and Ohio canal and the Baltimore & Ohio railroad. It was this belief that has kept life in the old waterway, life sustained by the Baltimore and Ohio Railroad company to bar out any possible rival," the *Cumberland Evening Times* reported.

The 60-mile extension line began in Big Pool and moved west toward Cumberland.

"Though the route lay entirely in the Potomac River Valley, the going was far from easy, since the Baltimore and Ohio Railroad, the Chesapeake and Ohio Canal, and the National Turnpike had already been built on the best routes. Thus, Western Maryland needed twenty-three bridges to cross the Potomac River, five streams, the C&O Canal, the B&O Railroad and three county roads," Roger Cook and Karl Zimmerman wrote in *The Western Maryland Railway*.

A tunnel through the mountain was one of the needed improvements that the Western Maryland needed to make to connect the Western Maryland railroad at Cherry Run with the West Virginia Central railroad at Cumberland. The plan was to connect these railroads with the Wabash Railroad in the Midwest and turn the Wabash into a transcontinental system.

A few minutes after the whistles and bells sounded in Paw Paw, someone pushed an electric button to trigger the explosion.

"There was a deep, rumbling report, the whole earth seemed to rock as though shaken by an earthquake and tones of rock plunged forward and toppled over into the canal and river," the *Cumberland Evening Times* reported.

The feared destruction of the town didn't happen. In fact, no loose rock flew more than 100 feet away from the mountain, but 20,000 cubic yards of rock was torn away from the mountain. The explosion was deemed a great success. It had accomplished what was needed with no unnecessary destruction.

The extension from Big Pool to Cumberland was proving to be very costly because of the number of bridges and tunnels that needed to be built along it. The Western Maryland Railway had 2,629 men, 300 animals, nine locomotives and 9 steam shovels building the extension. The average cost per mile was $100,000 (about $4 million today).

The extension was completed in 1906 and opened March 15. However, the railroad never became part of a transcontinental Wabash system. The Western Maryland Railway continued to service Allegany County until the Chessie System absorbed it in the mid-1970s.

A Forgotten Appendage of the WMRR

The Emmitsburg Railroad was not the mammoth project that the Western Maryland Railroad was. It ran from Emmitsburg, Md., to Rocky Ridge, Md., where it connected to the Western Maryland Railroad. The Emmitsburg Railroad traveled just a just short distance of seven miles.

Plans for building the railroad began in 1868. Many of Emmitsburg's leading citizens supported the incorporation of the railroad. When the Western Maryland Railroad reached Mechanicstown (Thurmont) in 1871, the board of directors for the Emmitsburg Railroad decided to connect to the Western Maryland Railroad at Rocky Ridge.

"In addition to Mount Saint Mary's, both the Daughters of Charity and the institution they operated, Saint Joseph's College, benefited from the Emmitsburg Railroad. At the announcement of the project to connect Emmitsburg to the Western Maryland Railroad, the Catholic Sisters at St. Joseph's acted with enthusiasm. This is evident in that they 'provided more than half the necessary capital and accordingly became the majority bond holders of the railroad… [likewise becoming] the only group of women to ever own a railroad'," Joe Ritz wrote in his article "The Last Train to Emmitsburg" for the Greater Emmitsburg Area Historical Society.

The project got underway the same year when John Donoghue started the grading. It was completed the next year, but a required bridge over Toms Creek wasn't finished until the November 1875.

"What a day that must have been! It was the day the citizens of Emmitsburg had looked forward to with great anticipation. It was a big day indeed, with free excursion over the line for everyone. The first excursion train from Emmitsburg to Baltimore was run on November 27, 1875, when over 400 passengers purchased tickets to make the trip. The first mail was handled over the road December 6, of that same year," Thurmont Historian George Wireman wrote about the railroad.

The Western Maryland Railroad operated the Emmitsburg Railroad for its first four years as the Emmitsburg Railroad directors worked out the kinks in running a railroad and built up a business that could support itself. The Emmitsburg Railroad Company took over operation of the line in 1879 and purchased its first engine.

A new life

The Emmitsburg Railroad continued running and growing until it hit a snag in 1897. It wasn't able to pay the interest on its debt and so it wound up being sold at auction in Frederick for $29,500.

The new owners reorganized and began rebuilding the railroad. An iron bridge replaced the wooden one. Heavier rails replaced the lighter rails. New ballast was laid.

"But this wasn't all! New motive power was purchased and the rolling stock was renovated. The depots were completely rebuilt. To better serve the customers of the Emmitsburg railroad, a new grain elevator and coal chutes were constructed at the south end of the community. Without question, things were really looking up for this little railroad. All employees, from the top office down, were dedicated to their jobs and took great pride in their work. In addition to all the improvements mentioned above, the railroad was proud to announce that it was now in a position to begin playing a small dividend of 2 percent to its stockholders. Yes, the future of the railroad looked very bright indeed," Wireman wrote.

A 1906 charter change by the Maryland State Legislature allowed the Emmitsburg Railroad to extend in any direction and gave railroad officials the ability to buy, lease or consolidate with any other company deemed necessary. The idea was to extend the railroad from Rocky Ridge to Woodsboro, Md., and connect with the Pennsylvania Railroad.

"On most runs, the train consisted of the engine and a combination baggage and passenger car. Sometimes a freight, cattle or coal car would be added, the addition of which, more often than not, would be a little too much weight for the engine, resulting a slowdown or even a complete stop along the way," William Hays wrote in his article, "The End of the Emmitsburg Road."

The engine for the Emmitsburg Railroad train at the engine house. Photo courtesy of the Western Maryland Railway Historical Society.

The high point

The 1909 homecoming celebration in Emmitsburg was also a boost for the railroad. Lots of excursions at special prices were scheduled. "Records show that during this week long celebration the railroad carried more passengers than at any time in its history. ...The celebration was a very big success and because of the many extra trains that were scheduled, the Emmitsburg Railroad was forced into renting additional cars from the Western Maryland Railroad," Wireman wrote.

As the country's roads became better and cars became more affordable and dependable, the age of railroads faded. That could be seen quite evidently with the Emmitsburg Railroad. Why walk to the railroad station, wait for the train, sit through the various stops just to make a seven-mile journey to Rocky Ridge? It was much easier to walk out of your house, get in a car and drive the distance in a shorter time. Even freight became cheaper to haul over roads without rails.

"However, when an increase in transportation technology occurred due to Henry Ford's concept of mass-producing automobiles, the need for passenger service trains greatly diminished. This obviously affected the railroad in Emmitsburg. In addition, the railroad had to cope with the bus service provided by Blue Ridge Bus Lines in 1931," Ritz wrote.

The Maryland Public Service Commission finally weighed in on the matter and said passenger service for the railroad would end June 4, 1935.

Even Mother Nature seemed to be against the railroad. The blizzard of 1936 damaged the railroad and the company couldn't afford the repair costs.

End of the line

Operating "when needed" is not an economical way to

run a business, which the railroad board of directors soon found out.

"When the official announcement was made that the Emmitsburg Railroad was closing for good on May 15, 1940, rail buffs from across the eastern portion of the United States converged upon Emmitsburg, hoping to get an opportunity to ride the last passenger train. Others came just to take a few pictures of what was left of the seven-mile line and its equipment," Wireman wrote.

However, Ritz wrote that he felt the railroad could have been saved, "Simply stated, its demise could have been prevented. It was a community project and many times during its brief history, the citizens of Emmitsburg, including various individuals and large religious organizations, did all they could to keep it running. As it was nearing its 'end', the Emmitsburg Railroad should have witnessed this same level of support from its community. With this realization, the Emmitsburg Railroad could have endured and continued serving the town with pride."

The railroad board of directors met in February 1940 and decided it was time to close down the railroad. The last day of service was May 15, 1940.

The rail line was sold at auction in August and then torn up the following year.

Sneaking Into Pennsylvania Without a Charter

One of the early goals of the Western Maryland Railroad was to reach Hagerstown and Williamsport in Washington County, Maryland. Williamsport, in particular, would have been an attractive destination. At that point, coal from the Chesapeake & Ohio Canal boats could have been offloaded onto rail cars to go to Baltimore. This would have allowed the railroad to compete for coal against the Baltimore & Ohio Railroad, which reached Cumberland in 1842 and had continued westward.

In 1864, Joseph S. Gitt conducted three studies on behalf of the railroad to evaluate routes from Union Bridge, Md., to Hagerstown. These were called the Mechanicstown route, the Emmitsburg route, and the "Middle" routes. For two years, railroad officials debated the best way to traverse Catoctin Mountain and South Mountain to reach Hagerstown.

"In this confused period, proposed routes were changed almost daily," Harold A. Williams wrote in *The Western Maryland Railway Story*.

As the railroad company prepared to ask for construction bids, John Lee Chapman, the mayor of Baltimore, got an injunction against the Western Maryland Railroad to "restrain the company from giving out, or consummating the contract." The City of Baltimore was a large stockholder in the railroad, and as such, could approve or veto, and proposed route. Chapman favored the middle route, but when opinion moved away from it, he got the injunction to stall the process.

The Mechanicstown Route was selected and the railroad reached the town in 1871. Now, the railroad faced the tougher problem of crossing Catoctin and South mountains. The best option was for the railroad to pass into Pennsylvania near Emmitsburg, Md., for a short distance. In essence, this route would allow the railroad to go around the steepest parts of the mountain.

This solution had its own problem, though. The Pennsylvania legislature had adopted a law that in order to get a charter in the state, the Western Maryland Railroad would need to pass the Waynesboro Turnpike at Liberty Mills, which was about 1.5 miles north of Emmitsburg, and the Gettysburg Railroad (the Gettysburg would not come under the control of the Western Maryland Railroad until 1909) would be allowed to connect to the Western Maryland Railroad at a point in Pennsylvania.

Chapman, who had become president of the railroad in 1866 while he was still mayor of Baltimore wrote, "This action would have compelled us, by going into Pennsylvania, to lengthen our Road some six or seven miles over our present route, to avoid the State of Pennsylvania entirely."

The Western Maryland Railroad directors wanted to stay in Maryland to avoid the complications that being in Pennsylvania would create. Variations on the proposed routes were considered.

Chapman described the final route, writing, ... it will pass through Middleburg and within five miles of Taneytown, Johnsville and Woodsborough, within six miles of Emmittsburg, and within two miles of Creagerstown, through Graceham and Mechanicstown, and within three miles of Catoctin Furnace, and then passing up Owings' Creek Valley, where Iron Ore abounds in the line of the Road, passing through Harbaugh Valley it reaches the summit of the Blue Ridge, which crosses within one mile of Monterey Springs, and within six miles of Waynesboro. It then passes down Germantown Valley, taking the west side of Mount Misery, through Smithsburg and Cavetown to Hagerstown."

While theoretically feasible, financially, it would stretch the railroad's resources, but for the railroad to survive, it needed to push further west. However, this created some short-term issues between the railroad and the contractors over costs. Also, the city of Baltimore got another injunction to stop the extension from Hagerstown to Williamsport because of the cost to the city as a shareholder. Besides, the city already had coal coming into the city along the B&O, so having the Western Maryland Railroad bring it in from Williamsport represented no gain for the city.

These issues were eventually worked out, construction continued and reached Sabillasville, Md., on Catoctin Mountain on August 28, 1871.

The railroad's annual report for 1871 noted that the railroad had run into additional construction problems beyond scaling a mountain. "Almost insurmountable difficulties have been overcome in the removal of the hard copper rock by the contractor in his progress through the rockcuts approaching Blue Ridge or Monterey Summit."

Since this was before dynamite was used for blasting, the copper rock formations did present an insurmountable problem. Removing them with black powder would have been dangerous and perhaps created other problems with the topography.

The engineers returned to their maps to try and figure out an affordable way around the problem, and once again, they looked to the north and Pennsylvania.

With this seeming to be the only feasible solution, they had to study a way to make the restrictions created by the Pennsylvania legislature feasible.

The solution found a loophole in Pennsylvania law and got the railroad around the copper formations. It was determined that the railroad only needed to go into Pennsylvania for a few hundred years. The company purchased farmland along the border and then ran their tracks across private property, which did not necessitate them needing a charter from Pennsylvania.

It was a cheaper solution that got the railroad around the worst part of the mountain and back on track to Hagerstown.

With some creative thinking, the railroad continued west and reached Hagerstown in 1872.

When the WMRR Caught a Tapeworm

In early 1899, the Western Maryland Railroad completed its western extension of the Baltimore and Harrisburg Division. The line went from Orrtanna, Pa., about eight miles west of Gettysburg, Pa., to the Highfield Station in Washington County, Maryland. Its winding route practically followed the route of "The Tapeworm."

The Tapeworm wasn't the parasite, but its route reminded people of one. Its winding path made its way over South Mountain, and those twists and turns earned it the nickname, "The Tapeworm." It was planned to be the Gettysburg Extension of the Pennsylvania Main Line, but that did not happen.

"It's the first railroad that got very far," says Bradley Hoch, author of "Thaddeus Stevens in Gettysburg: The Making of an Abolitionist."

"Far" is a relative term in this context because no train ever traveled on the Tapeworm, and no rails were ever laid. However, the route was surveyed and graded in Adams County, Pennsylvania, which is further than two earlier railroads got.

Fast track to "economic development?"

In the early decades of the 19th century, the railroad was the newest mode of transportation. Though a new technology, it held a lot of promise. Passengers could travel faster than they could in a wagon on a toll road, and they weren't dependent on a steady, flowing water source like a canal needed.

The construction of the Mauch Chunk Switchback Railroad in 1827 in Jim Thorpe, Pa., showed the country how useful railroads could be. The following year, the more ambitious Baltimore and Ohio Railroad broke ground in Baltimore.

"The Pennsylvania legislature chartered seventeen railroads in the next three years, and in the 1830s authorized 136 more lines—only 20 percent of which were actually built. Every community, it seemed, believed that prosperity was just around the corner—if only a railroad came its way," according to ExplorePAHistory.com.

Pennsylvania state representative Thaddeus Stevens and the Adams County business community also thought that way. "Thaddeus Stevens and Adams County wanted to jump on the bandwagon because they saw the railroad as a means of economic development for the area," Hoch wrote.

Stevens, a Gettysburg lawyer, would eventually become known as a staunch abolitionist and a supporter of free education. He had shown also that he wasn't opposed to some "sleight of hand and skullduggery" to get what he wanted. He was first elected to the Pennsylvania Assembly in 1833, and he began working toward getting a railroad to come through Adams County, no matter what it took.

When the Second National Bank in Philadelphia was seeking a state charter to stay viable, the bank was willing to pay the commonwealth a lot of money to ensure that it happened. When the charter came before Stevens' committee in the state legislature, he had written into it that the Canal Committee would survey a railroad from Gettysburg to a location west of Williamsport, Md., where it would connect to the Chesapeake and Ohio Canal. Also, he had added that the bank would pay $200,000 (about $8 million in today's dollars) for this.

"Stevens was able to weasel $200,000 out of the bank and the legal authority to spend it on a railroad," Hoch says.

Thaddeus Stevens, courtesy of Wikimedia Commons.

The Tapeworm

The Pennsylvania Legislature approved the charter on February 18, 1836. The surveying of a route over the mountains and south into Maryland began. Stevens' less-than-transparent methods earned him lots of critics who were quick to point out that the Gettysburg Extension of the Pennsylvania Main Line did more to make contractors rich, create unnecessary jobs, and buy votes than it did to create a viable rail line.

The final route selected was very serpentine (it took 35 miles to travel 18 miles between Stevens' Maria Furnace near Fairfield, Pa., and the Main Line). Stevens' critics dubbed the convoluted railroad, The Tapeworm. It apparently needed to be a winding route to get over the mountain without the use of an inclined plane. Using the surveyed route, trains should have been able to pull 90 tons of freight up the mountain at 10 miles per hour without the use of an inclined plane.

Stevens was criticized that the twisting route was laid out to benefit his iron furnace. Hoch points out that Stevens owned three iron furnaces at different times. Two were in the Caledonia area, and one was near Fairfield. The Tapeworm route ran through the Maria Furnace property near Fairfield. However, that furnace ceased operation in 1837.

Hoch says that Stevens would have benefitted from the railroad, but it would have been in the same way that any business near the track would have. Transportation costs would have been lowered for those businesses, and they would have become more competitive with other businesses that were located near transportation lines.

End of the line

In 1838, Democrats took control of the state legislature in a bitterly contested election that saw armed Democrats marching on the state house. Stevens found himself in the minority party and lost much of his support for the railroad.

"Laborers and masons picked up their tools and walked away from the Stevens' only partially built line, leaving embankments, cuts and fills, and bridges unfinished," according to ExplorePAHistory.com.

Stevens, as a canal commissioner, had also authorized the government to spend much more than budgeted for the project. The 63-mile line had been estimated to cost $750,000 (about $25.2 million in today's dollars) to survey and grade and $400,000 (about $13.5 million in today's dollars) to lay track. "Pennsylvania spent $750,000 on the initial miles of grading, and never laid an inch of track," Hoch says.

The final cost was $766,127 with (about $25.8 million in today's dollars) very little to show for the expenditure.

When the property was offered for sale in 1842, no buyers came forward. It wasn't until 1853 that the Western Maryland Railroad took over the property, and they didn't do anything with it until 1885 when a line using much of the Tapeworm route was built to Orrtanna and then Highfield Station.

"I searched, but I could not find any evidence that any money changed hands when the Western Maryland Railroad took over the property," Hoch wrote. "It looks like they may have been given it."

Stevens eventually overcame the stain the Tapeworm had on his reputation. He was elected to Congress in 1849 where he began to earn a national reputation. However, even as a congressman, he was a consistent supporter of railroads.

Although the Tapeworm Railroad was never built, Hoch says there is evidence that the graded route "may have acted as a trail or guide for the Underground Railroad." He was given a tour years ago of some of the houses that would have been near the Tapeworm had it been built. Inside these homes, he was shown hidden rooms where slaves traveling on the Underground Railroad could have hidden.

Today, there are still remnants of the railroad that can be seen in Adams County. Perhaps the best known is the McPherson Ridge railway cut, which was the location of some of the first day's fighting during the Battle of Gettysburg. Other artifacts that remain are a single-arch bridge over Toms Creek near Iron Springs, a viaduct at Virginia Mills, a cut near Marsh Creek, a rail bed near Willoughby Run, and the Seminary Ridge railway cut.

The McPherson Ridge Railroad Cut in Gettysburg is one of the few improvements that remain from the Tapeworm Railroad. This railroad cut was eventually taken over by other railroads including the Western Maryland Railway. Photo courtesy of Wikimedia Commons.

Openings & Closings

Bits and Pieces Make the Whole

The Western Maryland Railway was not simply built from point A to point B like its sister line, the Baltimore and Ohio Railroad. The Western Maryland was built through the incorporation of smaller railroads, some of which were created through the consolidation of even smaller railroads.

In some cases, the smaller railroads maintained their original name because the Western Maryland Railway only operated it or managed it. Once the Western Maryland Railway purchased them, the name was changed to the Western Maryland Railway.

Here is a list of how those smaller railroads came together to form the great Western Maryland Railway pulled together from the Western Maryland Railway Historical Society, History of the Western Maryland Railway, and online sources.

The Baltimore, Carroll and Frederick Railroad formed the first link in the chain. Chartered in 1852, it was renamed the following year to the Western Maryland Rail Road Company. Its original goal was to build a line from the terminus of the Baltimore and Susquehanna Railroad's Green Spring Branch to the headwaters of the Monocacy, which would have been around Rocky Ridge or Mechanicstown (Thurmont) in Maryland. With the name change in 1853, its ultimate goal was extended to reach Hagerstown.

In 1857, the Western Maryland Rail Road Company purchased the **Green Spring Branch of the Northern Central Railway** from Relay House to Owings Mills, Maryland.

The **Hanover Branch Railroad** was incorporated in 1847 and built between Hanover and Hanover Junction in Pennsylvania. The Western Maryland Railroad took control of it in 1886.

The Western Maryland Railway's largest period of growth began in 1904 when it became part of the Fuller Syndicate. This was also when the railroad changed its name once again. This time, the Western Maryland Railroad became the Western Maryland Railway.

The **Piedmont and Cumberland Railway** incorporated in 1886, and the Western Maryland Railway took it over in 1904.

The **Potomac Valley Railroad** incorporated in 1891, and the Western Maryland Railway took it over in 1904.

The **Belington and Beaver Creek Railroad** incorporated in 1899 to build from Belington, West Virginia, to Weaver, West Virginia, and the Western Maryland Railway took it over in 1904.

The **Coal and Iron Railway** incorporated in 1899, and the Western Maryland Railway took it over in 1904.

The **Potomac and Piedmont Coal and Railroad** incorporated in Maryland in 1866. It became part of the **West Virginia Central and Pittsburgh Railway** in 1881. This railroad was chartered to build from any point on the B&O Railroad along the North Branch Potomac River to any of the area's coal mines. The Western Maryland acquired it in 1905.

The **Western Maryland Tidewater Rail Road** was incorporated in 1883. It became part of the Western Maryland Railway in 1905.

The **Connellsville and State Line Railway** incorporated in 1910 to build the Connellsville Extension between Cumberland, Maryland, and Connellsville, Pennsylvania. The Western Maryland Railway began operating it upon completion in 1912.

The **Hagerstown and State Line Railroad** was incorporated in 1884. The **Washington and Franklin Railroad**, which incorporated in 1898 to build from Quinsonia, Pennsylvania, to Zumbro, Pennsylvania, acquired the line in 1899. The Western Maryland Railway began using some of the Washington and Franklin Railroad lines in 1915.

The **Williamsport, Nessle and Martinsburg Railway** incorporated in 1913. The Western Maryland Railway began operating it upon its completion in 1915.

The **Somerset Coal Railway** incorporated in 1915 to build from Coal Junction to Bell and Gray to Gray Junction in Pennsylvania. The Western Maryland Railway operated it from the start.

The Emmitsburg Railroad engine. Photo courtesy of the Western Maryland Railway Historical Society.

The **Chesapeake and Curtis Bay Railroad** incorporated in 1915. The Western Maryland Railway began operating it in 1916 and purchased it in 1927.

Fairmont Helen's Run Railway incorporated in 1915,

and the Western Maryland Railway took it over in 1916.

The **Gettysburg Railroad,** which ran from Gettysburg to Hanover, was incorporated in 1851. It became part of the **Susquehanna, Gettysburg and Potomac Railway** in 1871. It was reorganized as the **Hanover Junction, Hanover and Gettysburg Railroad** in 1874 and merged into the **Baltimore and Harrisburg Railway** in 1886. The Western Maryland acquired the Baltimore and Harrisburg Railway in 1917.

The **Bachman Valley Railroad** incorporated in 1871 and began by hauling iron ore from nearby mines. It was reorganized as the Hanover Junction, Hanover and Gettysburg Railroad in 1874 and merged into the Baltimore and Harrisburg Railway in 1886. The Western Maryland acquired the Baltimore and Harrisburg Railway in 1917.

In 1876, the **Pennsylvania Railroad** incorporated in Maryland to build a line from Cumberland to Ellerslie, where it connected to the Pennsylvania Railroad in Pennsylvania. It merged with the **Georges Creek and Cumberland Railroad** (incorporated in 1876) in 1888. The Western Maryland Railway began operating the Georges Creek and Cumberland Railroad in 1913, and a full merger was completed in 1917.

The **Baltimore and Hanover** Railroad was incorporated in 1877. The Hanover Junction, Hanover and Gettysburg Railroad operated it. It became part of the Baltimore and Harrisburg Railway in 1886. The Western Maryland acquired the Baltimore and Harrisburg Railway in 1917.

The **Baltimore and Cumberland Valley Railroad** was incorporated in 1878 to build from Edgemont, Maryland, to Waynesboro, Pennsylvania. When it built its line from Waynesboro to Shippensburg, Pennsylvania, the Western Maryland Railway began leasing the line in 1881. The Western Maryland Railway acquired it in 1917.

The **Fairmont Bingamon Railway** was incorporated in 1916 to build from Hutchinson to Wyatt, both in West Virginia, and the Western Maryland acquired it in 1917.

The **Greenbrier and Elk River Railroad** incorporated in 1891 to run from Cass, West Virginia, to Spruce, West Virginia. The West Virginia Pulp and Paper Company acquired it in 1909 and expanded it under a new charter as the **Greenbrier, Cheat and Elk Railroad** in 1910. The Western Maryland Railway acquired it in 1927.

A train derailment on the Western Maryland Railway. Photo courtesy of Western Maryland's Historical Library.

The **Chaffee Railroad** incorporated in 1904 as a Western Virginia coal railroad. The Western Maryland Railway acquired it in 1929.

The **Cumberland and Pennsylvania Railroad**, which had been purchased in 1944, was merged into the Western Maryland Railway in 1953.

That is a total of 29 railroads that make up the Western Maryland Railway. It should also be understood that throughout these acquisitions and mergers, the Western Maryland was continuing to build out its own line. Beginning in Baltimore at the east, it reached as far west as Wyatt in the west. It went as far north as Coal Junction in Pennsylvania and as far south as Laurel Bank in West Virginia. These mergers and acquisitions allowed the Western Maryland Railway to grow from a regional railroad in Maryland into a major rail line.

Although it had fought off some earlier attempts of larger companies to take it over, the Western Maryland Railway eventually became part of the **Chessie System** in the 1970s, which became **CSX Transportation** in the 1980s.

At the end, the Western Maryland Railway was a jigsaw puzzle that completed with all the pieces fitting together properly.

The Western Maryland Railway station in Cumberland, MD. Photo courtesy of the Western Maryland Historical Library.

Railroads that made up the Western Maryland Railway by year they were acquired

1852

- The Baltimore, Carroll and Frederick Railroad

1857

- Green Spring Branch of the Northern Central Railway

1886

- Hanover Branch Railroad

1904

- Belington and Beaver Creek Railroad
- Coal and Iron Railway
- Piedmont and Cumberland Railway
- Potomac Valley Railroad

1905

- Potomac and Piedmont Coal and Railroad
- West Virginia Central and Pittsburgh Railway
- Western Maryland Tidewater Rail Road

1910

- Connellsville and State Line Railway

1915

- Hagerstown and State Line Railroad
- Somerset Coal Railway
- Washington and Franklin Railroad
- Williamsport, Nessle and Martinsburg Railway

1916

- Chesapeake and Curtis Bay Railroad
- Fairmont Helen's Run Railway

1917

- Bachman Valley Railroad
- Baltimore and Cumberland Valley Railroad
- Baltimore and Hanover Railroad
- Baltimore and Harrisburg Railway
- Fairmont Bingamon Railway
- Georges Creek and Cumberland Railroad
- Gettysburg Railroad
- Hanover Junction, Hanover and Gettysburg Railroad
- Pennsylvania Railroad
- Susquehanna, Gettysburg and Potomac Railway

1927

- Greenbrier and Elk River Railroad
- Greenbrier, Cheat and Elk Railroad

1929

- Chaffee Railroad

1953

- Cumberland and Pennsylvania Railroad

Thurmont Loses Its Railroad Station

One of the reasons that there is a Thurmont was lost in 1967.

Thurmont was originally called Mechanicstown, but a movement in the early 1890s started to come up with a more progressive name for the town that was growing because it was a stop along the Western Maryland Railroad. Among the supporters of a name change were the railroad directors.

"The railroad was all for the idea since it would relieve the shipping and passenger problems caused by a profusion of the 'sound alike' communities. There was Mechanicsburg and Mechanicsville, Pennsylvania, and several Mechanicsvilles in Maryland as well as our town," according to *A Thurmont Scrapbook.*

The Western Maryland Railroad had first reached Mechanicstown on January 9, 1871. The first stationmaster was Harry Shriner.

"Upon the event of the coming of the railroad to Mechanicstown, a group of civic-minded citizens arranged a reception and a banquet for the railroad officials and their guests. It was a big event, taking place in the Stocksdale Warehouse located beside the tracks at the end of Carroll Street," George Wireman wrote in the *Catoctin Enterprise* in 1972.

The warehouse served as a temporary depot for the telegrapher and expressman until a permanent depot could be built on the site of the old cannery in Thurmont. The depot had two waiting rooms, an office for the stationmaster and telegrapher, and sanitary facilities. The grounds outside were landscaped, and there was a water tank at either end of the depot.

By 1890, six passenger, mail and express trains (three eastbound and three westbound) ran through Thurmont daily.

In 1914, Thurmont even had a milk service train running to Baltimore.

The Western Maryland Railway Station in Thurmont, Md., as a train is pulling in. Photo courtesy of Thurmontimages.com.

During 1923, a young man named S. Elmer Barnhart started working for the Western Maryland Railway. He was a fresh graduate of the Dodge Institute of Telegraphy and State Agency in Valparaiso, Indiana. He had been born in Greencastle, Pennsylvania, and served in France with Base Hospital 98 during World War I.

He began his career with the railroad at Edgemont, Maryland, but he soon moved to the Rocky Ridge, Maryland, station.

"Part of his job involved relaying basketball results by

Morse telegraphy from Mt. St. Mary's College to the Associated Press," George May wrote in the *Frederick Post* in 1967.

Barnhart took over operating the Thurmont station in September 1939.

"The peak of his career was in 1952 when he was freight, ticket and baggage agent and operator at Thurmont; agent for the Railway Express Agency; Mayor of Thurmont which included being superintendent of the Municipal Light Company and Chief of Police and an elder and financial secretary of St. John's Lutheran Church of Thurmont," May wrote.

As automobiles continued to gain favor as a form of transportation for Americans, the Western Maryland Railway stopped passenger service to Thurmont on March 1, 1957. Freight and mail service continued, though.

Occasionally, a few special trains would be scheduled to carry passengers on special excursions, usually to Pen-Mar Park.

"On Saturday, October 12, 1963, the local station resembled a scene from the pages of history when large crowds gathered to ride the special excursions to Pen Mar Park, located a short distance west of Blue Ridge Summit in the beautiful Blue Ridge Mountains," Wireman wrote.

With little notice, the Western Maryland Railway closed the Thurmont depot on January 13, 1967.

"The need for the station diminished during recent years because of more modern accounting practices in Hagerstown, which took over the work of the Thurmont Agency," Wireman wrote.

Many people assume that the decision to close the depot came about because Barnhart retired on January 1, 1967, at age 65. He had spent 44 years with the railroad and 27 years in charge of the Thurmont train station.

"On April 4, 1967, the fate of the station was soon

learned. A wrecking crew appeared on the scene and began demolishing this Heritage Landmark. Within the short period of three days, a stranger visiting the site would never have realized that a railroad station once stood on this very spot," Wireman wrote.

While the trains still run through Thurmont, they no longer stop in the town.

Putting Shovel to the Ground

T he railroad that would eventually become one of the major rail operations in the region started out with little fanfare or celebration.

"Ground was broken, without ceremony, on July 11, 1857," Harold A. Williams wrote in *The Western Maryland Railway Story*. Edward M. Killough's *History of the Western Maryland Railroad*, the other major work on the history of the railroad, doesn't even mention the event.

That's because it had been a long journey to reach the point to break ground, even to the point that the railroad's original name was changed before the railroad even started being built. The Western Maryland Railway was originally chartered in May 1852 as the Baltimore, Carroll & Frederick Rail Road Company and renamed shortly thereafter.

Less than a year after its chartering, which is considered the company's birthday, enough money had been pledged through subscriptions that the company could be organized on February 14, 1853. Directors were elected, and the first reports of the meeting showed there was a disagreement about how construction should proceed.

The Baltimore Sun noted with perhaps too much optimism, "Among other business transacted, provision was made for immediate new surveys of the routes, and it is said that if the weather is not too inclement, in the course of six weeks they will be sufficiently posted to be able to locate the road and put portions under contract."

Six weeks became six months, then a year, and finally on March 31, 1857, more than four years later, the first contracts were let.

In the meantime, a special act of the Maryland Legislature on March 21, 1853, renamed the railroad the Western Maryland Rail Road Company. The Baltimore, Carroll & Frederick Rail Road Company was no longer appropriate since the legislative act also allowed the company to issue bonds as it built its way west toward Hagerstown, Md.

Other issues continued to plague the company: acquiring and keeping the funding because of construction delays and deciding on the route the construction would follow.

Although no original construction was done during the first five years, the Western Maryland Railroad did acquire 10 miles of an abandoned Baltimore and Susquehanna Railroad line from Relay House to Owings Mills in Maryland.

Then in early 1857, the directors voted to accept the construction proposals from Irwin and Taylor, even though the railroad only had $271,250 of the projected $535,756 needed for construction. Despite this, the stockholders voted 1802 to 20 to begin construction.

The directors signed a contract on March 31, 1857, with Irwin and Taylor for bridging and grading land between Relay House and Union Bridge, Md., for $225,000.

Work began on the railroad on July 11. Given that the occasion was marked without ceremony, it is likely that the crew simply showed up that day and started work without any bands or speeches to mark the occasion. No known sources even mark where the groundbreaking started, although it was likely done at Owings Mills because that was the end of the old Baltimore and Susquehanna line and the destination was Westminster, Md.

No bunting flapped in the breeze, no mayor's speech echoed across the field. The "groundbreaking" was just another workday. Laborers, many of them Irish immigrants, some free Black men, and a few local farmhands between harvests, stood in small knots, shovels and picks over their shoulders.

The work involved cutting into hillsides, clearing trees, and laying the first sections of roadbed and building any bridges that were needed to cross rivers and culverts. A major crossing would have been the Patapsco River on the border between Baltimore and Carroll counties. It was manual work done with picks, shovels, and mule teams pulling scrapers.

There was no ribbon cut, no photographer, no celebratory banquet. Only the scrape of shovels, the grunt of mules, and the slow advance of the grading crews westward—anonymous men beginning a line that will one day run from tidewater to the Alleghenies.

Although there was no ceremony, it was an important event because it marked the first tangible evidence that a railroad would be built.

By August, seventy men were working on grading the roadbed, consisting of two gangs of men; one working between Groff's Mills, Md., and Reisterstown, Md., and the other between Union Bridge and New Windsor, Md.

The start of work also gave subscriptions a boost as people could see work was started and wanted to be a part of it.

The rail line reached Westminster in July 1861 and Union Bridge in November 1862.

Western Maryland Railroad's First Park

Before the Western Maryland Railroad built Pen-Mar Park on South Mountain, it built another park closer to Baltimore that didn't attract as much attention. Greenwood Park was built nine miles from Fulton Station in Baltimore County. It was built in 1875, three years before Pen-Mar began attracting thousands of visitors a year.

The Western Maryland Railroad leased land that contained a beautiful grove from C. L. Rogers for a 10-year period. The railroad then built 1,500 feet of track from the main line to the new park to bring visitors to the park. A pavilion, a restaurant, a lake for boating, swings, fountains, and other attractions were constructed to attract people from Baltimore City for a day's outing.

What made the park workable as an attraction was that the year before newly elected Western Maryland Railroad President John Mifflin Hood had entered into a contract with the Baltimore and Potomac Railroad to use their tunnel. This allowed the Western Maryland Railroad to reach Union Station and Hillen Station in Baltimore City.

The Baltimore and Potomac Railroad, which opened in 1872, connected Baltimore to Washington, D.C. It was owned and operated by the Pennsylvania Railroad. The 800-foot-long tunnel in the northwest section of the city was built after the Baltimore and Potomac was granted a right-of-way through the city. The tunnel, which ran under Winchester Street and Wilson Street, opened on June 29, 1873.

However, this new section of the Western Maryland Railroad didn't start using the tunnel until after the park opened.

Greenwood Park brought a surge of new visitors who wanted to escape the heat and humidity of the city for a relaxing day in the country. To reach the park, they traveled on the Western Maryland Railroad, which brought them right to the park.

During the park's first year in operation, Hood said, "Already the patronage has greatly exceeded our expectations and it is found that the company can successfully compete with the steamboats at their prices, with a very satisfactory margin of profit."

Encouraged by the success of Greenwood Park, the railroad built Pen-Mar Park. The mountain park seemed to suck the oxygen out of the room as the railroad focused its attention on making Pen-Mar a destination, perhaps because they could charge more for a ticket for the longer journey to reach the park, and it was more likely to be a place where people stayed for more than a day.

Hood wrote in an annual report, "The summer travel on your road has now reached such proportions as to demand more extended hotel and boarding house accommodations, and it is hoped that the citizens along the line will find it pleasant as well as profitable to provide for the patronage of thousands who are ready and anxious to avail themselves of any opportunities that are offered for a summer sojourn in a country so eminently suited to their wants."

According to *The Western Maryland Railway Story* by Harold A. Williams, the pavilion in Pen-Mar was actually the pavilion from Greenwood, which was disassembled and rebuilt at Pen-Mar.

When the Greenwood Park land lease ended in 1885, it was used very little, and the lease was not renewed.

The Western Maryland Comes to Mechanicstown

Thurmont's stop on the Western Maryland Railway makes up only a paragraph in the history of the railroad. For Thurmont, Maryland, however, it was a major event that not only helped shape the town's future but also give it its unique name.

The Western Maryland Railway began in 1852 as the Baltimore, Carroll and Frederick Railroad. The goal at that time was to build a railroad from Baltimore to Washington County.

The Maryland General Assembly changed the name to the Western Maryland Rail Road Company the following year. For many years, the terminus of the railroad was at Union Bridge, where it reached in 1862.

However, this was not the goal of the railroad. The residents of Mechanicstown, Maryland, knew their town was along the proposed route of the railroad and wanted to see it completed as many other people did. The original charter in 1852 called for the railroad to be built to the headwaters of the Monocacy River, which meant that the terminus would be at Mechanicstown or Rocky Ridge, Maryland.

An 1871 article in the Catoctin Clarion noted, "May it not be said of the people of Mechanicstown that they have pinned their faith to the Western Maryland Railroad? This great artery of travel and commerce, hampered as it has been and still is, has done much for the section of the country through which it passes…"

Lobbying was begun to try and get construction to resume once more on the railroad and on February 24, 1872, the Catoctin Clarion announced, "Rejoice, people of Mechanicstown!" A vote had been taken a few days earlier in Baltimore that was overwhelmingly in favor of continuing the construction of the Western Maryland Railway to Hagerstown and beyond.

"This vote is the harbinger of a new era for this great enterprise," the newspaper reported.

The announcement brought with it some immediate economic activity in town. "Already on the strength of this news several parties in our town and vicinity have commenced sinking shafts in close proximity to the road for the discovery of ore and ore banks, which, we are persuaded, exist in quantities in our very midst," according to the newspaper. These speculators were searching for iron that could be smelted into pig iron at Catoctin Furnace and used for making rails.

When the railroad opened to Mechanicstown later in 1872, George Wireman wrote in *Gateway to the Mountains,* "a group of civic-minded citizens arranged a reception and a banquet for the railroad officials and their guests. This event took place in the local warehouse and a gala celebration was enjoyed by all who attended."

The depot was built on the site of an old cannery and a water tower was built just to the north of it. The Mechanicstown Station also had a freight yard and engine house.

The railroad brought so much business and travelers into the area that a new depot and associated facilities eventually had to be built near Carroll Street. "The new depot was built along the main line near Carroll Street and featured two waiting rooms, stationmaster and telegrapher's office and sanitary facilities. The grounds were graced with four large grass plots, one on the east, one on the west side of the station and two in front. These plots were beautified with ornamental grass and flowers protected by low guard rails. The front plots had large lawn vases in the center with blooming flowers," Wireman described the new depot.

Besides the increased business, the Western Maryland Railroad led to another major change on Mechanicstown in 1894. Because of the number of town along the line with names similar to Mechanicstown, the Post Office Department requested that the name be changed. Thurmont was chosen after much debate and a town vote.

The Western Maryland Railway served Thurmont until 1967 when the station closed.

Creating a Summer Playground

Col. John Mifflin Hood, president of the Western Maryland Railroad, created Pen-Mar Park in August 1877. The park offered a view of over 2,000 square miles and two mountain ranges at an altitude of 1,400 feet.

"From here on a clear day, one could see the town clock in Chambersburg, Pennsylvania, at a distance of 24 miles – with binoculars, of course," Frank and Suanne Woodring wrote in the book, *Images of America: Pen-Mar*.

Hood's interest in developing a summer resort is interesting since once be became president of the Western Maryland Railroad, he seldom took vacations himself and seemed to have given up his long-time hobby of fox hunting. His life became the railroad, running it, growing it, and making it better. His drive behind creating the park was that he knew it would increase ridership on the Western Maryland Railroad with people who wanted to get away from the cities.

To encourage the use of the Western Maryland Railroad to reach the park, the railroad's timetable noted, "Passengers are cautioned against using any conveyances excepting such as are recognized by the Railroad Co., whose drivers are indicated by badges."

In the days before air conditioning, summer heat and humidity made big cities like Baltimore and Washington D.C. nearly unbearable at times. Those who could would travel to summer homes in more-agreeable climes. It wasn't always possible for middle-class families and federal officials, though.

Pen-Mar Park on South Mountain, near the intersection

of four counties, featured a dancing pavilion and a dining room that could seat 450 people and offered 50 cent (about $15 today) chicken dinners. An observation tower was added in 1878. The very popular three-foot-high miniature railroad with an engine, tender, and three cars was added in 1904. As many of 2,000 people a day rode the Little Wabash around the park.

The children's playground at Pen-Mar Park. Photo courtesy of the Washington County Historical Society.

The park quickly became a popular destination for tourists who traveled on the special excursion train, the Blue Mountain Express, along the railroad from Baltimore to the Maryland and Pennsylvania mountains. Hagerstown, Maryland, served as another popular departure point for visitors to the park. The round-trip fare from Baltimore to the park was $1 (about $30 today) and took about three hours to reach the park.

"So popular was the Pen-Mar Express on Sundays and holidays during the summer that the Western Maryland sometimes had to borrow coaches from the Pennsylvania Railroad to accommodate the throngs going to Pen Mar," the Woodrings wrote.

The promenade at Pen-Mar Park. Photo courtesy of the Washington County Historical Society.

Its growing popularity also attracted visitors who arrived by other means to enjoy the park facilities.

The peak single-day attendance at the park was 20,000 people. During the season, the typical attendance at the park was between 4,000 and 5,000 people.

As its popularity grew, Hood "encouraged the construction of the Blue Mountain House, which was completely built in 1883 in seventy-six working days," Edward M. Killough wrote in History of the Western Maryland Railway. The hotel could house up to 400 guests.

The park's popularity also spurred the construction of other hotels and boarding houses that weren't owned by the railroad company.

By 1915, an effort started to turn Pen-Mar, Cascade, and the Blue Ridge Summit areas into a summer capital for federal officials and foreign diplomats.

In August, the Waynesboro (Pennsylvania) Board of Trade appointed a committee to open communications with Congressman D. K. Focht "and urge him to use his influence in having the summer capital located in this section," according to the *Gettysburg Times*.

The miniature train at Pen-Mar Park was a popular attraction for both children and adults. Photo courtesy of Wikimedia Commons.

W. H. Doll, of the traffic department of the Western Maryland Railway, traveled to Washington, D. C. and met with one of President Woodrow Wilson's secretaries to show the railroad's support for having Blue Ridge Summit be the summer capital.

In 1915, some of the towns surrounding the capital city began making their case to serve as the summer capital for the United States in a similar way to the way President Dwight D. Eisenhower would use his Gettysburg, Pennsylvania, home as a temporary White House while he was recovering from a heart attack. Another example, is the reason President Franklin D. Roosevelt chose Catoctin Mountain in Maryland as the site of his summer getaway, Shangri-La. These were towns within a couple hours of Washington and at a higher elevation that brought cooler, less humid air in the summers.

For a while, it seemed that the government was considering officially designating the town as the summer capital. Engineers from Washington traveled to Blue Ridge Summit in October to take elevations and measurements of town and surrounding area. Local officials took it as a sign that the government was collecting data on where to build government buildings.

It wasn't the first time towns had made an appeal to be the summer capital. Earlier in the year, Braddock Heights in Frederick County had made its case only to see nothing come of it. It doesn't seem that the town fathers made much of persuasive appeal other than offering cooler summer weather within a fairly close location to Washington, D.C.

Meanwhile Virginia Congressman Charles Carlin was making the case for the summer capital being in the Virginia mountains not far from Washington. The basis of his appeal was that he would submit a bill for designating a summer capital, but only if it was located in his district in Virginia.

Although Blue Ridge Summit's official recognition as the summer capital failed, the town continued to appeal to foreign delegations. Even as late as 1940, about a dozen foreign embassies maintained summer legations in Blue Ridge, many at Monterey, occasioning it to be called often "the summer capitol of the United States," according to the Living Places web page for the Monterey Historic District.

The Blue Mountain House was destroyed by fire in 1913. The Western Maryland Railway sold the park in 1930, and the park closed entirely in 1943.

Washington County, Maryland, opened a county park at the location in 1980. Although different in look, the lookout, picnic shelter, playground and pavilion have been reconstructed on the original sites.

Guests enjoyed delicious meals in the dining room at Pen-Mar Park. Photo courtesy of the New York Public Library.

TRAIN WRECKS

The Great Ransom Train Wreck of 1905

At 4:25 p.m. on Saturday, June 17, 1905, flagman George Lynch and the crew of a Western Maryland Railway freight, pulled onto a siding at Gorsuch, Maryland. Their eastbound train had to let three westbound trains pass.

"We all got down from the train and sat on a pile of ties near the track," he recalled in an article in the New York Times. "The two engineers and the conductors had their time cards and schedules and we talked for awhile about the time we were making, how long we had to wait for No. 5 and where we would run to after she passed."

Lynch's eighteen-car freight, drawn by Engines 41 and 43, was heavily laden with coal. Once the three westbound trains had gone by, the line would be open to Baltimore, but with only one set of tracks, someone had to wait, and the other trains had priority. The crew sat for "considerably" more than an hour. The Union Bridge Accommodation, No. 17, passed on time, as did the No. 11 Blue Mountain Express, also on time for its first trip of the season.

Lynch described what happened next to a newspaper reporter. With a few minutes left before the third westbound train, the No. 5 Thurmont Express, was scheduled to pass, Lynch left the group to get some water at a nearby spring. When he returned, the engineers were in their respective engines, and the firemen were shoveling coal into the fires to build up steam.

"Jump on board if you're going," one of the engineers called. The flagman looked at his watch once again. By his reckoning they had a few more minutes before the train could leave but, not wanting to be left behind, Lynch grabbed a handrail and pulled himself aboard as the train began to roll. He asked the fireman where they would pass the No. 5.

"At Lawndale," was the answer he thought he heard over the noise of the engine as the freight gathered speed.

The flagman instantly realized they did not have time to reach Lawndale and shouted, "For God's sake, look at your watch!"

Clearing the wreckage of the train wreck at Ransom, MD. Photo courtesy of Thurmontimages.com.

The fireman waved his hand as if nothing was wrong, prompting Lynch to think that his own watch needed adjustment. "There were two engineers, the two conductors, and the fireman, five in all, who had the time and knew the schedules as well as I did," he said later. Thurmont historian and train enthusiast George Wireman believed that the engineers or conductors did not know how many trains had already passed, "But how they could get so mixed up about ordinary work has been a question mark for years."

The Washington Post later suggested "that a new schedule goes into effect tomorrow [and] may have caused some confusion." The new schedule included a stop in Glyndon, and added nine minutes to the time the No. 5 had previously taken to reach Westminster. If the freight crew thought they were using the new schedule, the No. 5 would have been 4.5 miles farther east, giving them enough time to reach the Lawndale siding safely. Another possibility is that the crew of the freight was unaware that the Blue Mountain Express was making its first run of the season and were expecting two trains, not three. Yet according to Lynch's version of events, the crew knew a third train was coming and still thought they had time to pull onto the siding at Lawndale. Concerned about the time, Lynch also said he considered pulling down the air brakes but deferred to the greater experience of the other crewmen, according to an article in The Catoctin Clarion.

The No. 5, with approximately one hundred passengers on board, drew away from Hillen Station in Baltimore at 5 p.m. as scheduled. Hauling three passenger coaches and a baggage combination car, it traveled thirty miles per hour. A group of railroad workers, many of whom lived in Thurmont and Catoctin Furnace, rode in the last car. They had boarded the train at Mount Hope where they had been working to repair the damage from a small freight wreck the previous week. Overcrowding forced some to sit on the bumpers between the baggage car and the engine tender and between the baggage car and the first passenger car, Elizabeth Y. Anderson wrote in *Faith in the Furnace: A History of Harriet Chapel Catoctin Furnace, Maryland.*

Clearing the wreckage of the train wreck at Ransom, MD. Photo courtesy of Thurmontimages.com.

The collision

On the afternoon of June 17, 1905, thirteen-year-old Emil A. Caple was walking near the tracks on his way to the Patapsco post office and general store. He was expecting to see the Blue Mountain Express pass him heading west, not an eastbound freight.

"We thought it was strange to see the freight train passing through Patapsco, knowing it was almost time for the passenger train to arrive from Baltimore. But there was a siding in Lawndale where the telegraph operator in Westminster could have informed the passenger train operator to wait since the telegraph dispatchers were supposed to know the whereabouts of all trains at all times," Caple said in an interview in Neighborhoods of West Carroll.

At about 5:55 p.m., near Ransom, a little village southeast of Patapsco in Carroll County, the No. 5 and the freight train met head-on. "Just west of the bridge, they came together with terrific force, the three engines being piled one upon another, fortunately in such a manner that sufficient steam connections were broken, to relieve the boilers, and thus prevent the further horror of one or more explosions," the Washington Post reported. "After the freight train whizzed past Patapsco, it was only a couple of minutes and it sounded like the whole train rolled down the track," Caple remembered. "The noise was terrific! I never heard such an awful noise like that!"

George C. Buckingham was a conductor on the eastbound freight. He had just looked at his pocket watch and thought the train would be able to make up the five minutes it was running behind. As he put his watch back in his pocket, he felt "the awful plunging jar, crash and grind of wood and steel. … There was no time to move. The man ahead of me, a Washington doctor, dived out his window; we were two seats from the front of the first coach, and I sprang to my feet and amid the groans and shrieks of the injured, I made my way out," Buckingham told the Hagerstown Daily Mail.

The Frederick Daily News reported that the railroad men who were sitting on the bumper suffered the worst. "The more fortunate, who were on the engine, jumped or were thrown from the train and were only injured. Those in the baggage car were terribly mangled, and the crews of all three engines were killed. Their bodies all believed to be under the wreckage of the engines," reported The New York Times. Lynch, at the back of the train at the time of the collision, was the only survivor among the nine crew members on the three engines, "There was a jar and then a succession of bumps, but I was not thrown down," he said. "The three steam monsters were reduced to scrap iron," yet none of the passenger coaches derailed. With the exception of minor cuts and bruises, all of the travelers in the coaches survived uninjured, as reported by the Frederick Daily News.

Caple said that everyone who had heard the collision came running. "I ran right along with them as fast as my legs could carry me. On the way down, we passed a man with a railroad flag in his hand running towards the Patapsco store. Somebody asked him, 'What happened?' He said, 'My God, I don't know.' He ran up the track to telephone Westminster." When Caple arrived at Ransom, it was hard for him to see the actual wreck for all the steam escaping from mangled engines. What he did see, he wished he hadn't:

> People were crawling from the wreck scalded. Some were laying with arms and legs chopped off and screaming and crying were terrible. Carloads of lard in wooden barrels burst open and many passengers were covered with it and rescue crews had to work in it up to the knees to pull people out. They told all of us to either help or we would have to leave. So no matter what age, every one of us pitched in to help.
>
> I helped pick up arms and legs. No one knew for sure who they belonged to, so they told us to give them to anybody who didn't have one that it looked like they belonged to. I helped another man who was scalded. He kept crying that he was so cold, so I got a coat and put [it] over him. They said he had been scalded inside and I believe he died. The whole bottom just west of the Patapsco River was strewn with wreckage and bodies and people called for help.

Buckingham joined the other men working to remove the injured and dead from the wreckage. "We lifted and carried away all who lay about, trying to identify them through the blood and coal dirt, asking them their names and endeavoring to ascertain the extent of the damage," according to the Hagerstown Daily Mail.

Buckingham found the engineer on Engine 41, L. D. Rice, who was trapped because his feet were caught in twisted metal. "Shake my hand," Rice said, "for good bye, Captain, I am going fast." Buckingham told him to "Take that off your mind. We are going to get you out all right." By all appearances, Rice was not worried. Buckingham said he had a sad, but resigned expression on his face. "I know what I can stand. Why man, I am cooked, cooked in the steam." Rice must have been in shock by that point, and not reacting to the pain. However, with horror Buckingham noted that, "When I released my hand from his flesh, it came from the bone with mine."

Westminster learned of the crash minutes after it happened. Captain H. Clay Eby, formerly a conductor on one of the trains involved, lived near the site. Though he could not see the collision, he recognized the sound and what it meant. He had a telephone in his house and called E. O. Grimes, the railroad agent in Westminster, with the news. Grimes and his team sent out a relief train to take the injured to a hospital in Baltimore. "Just before the first relief train taking the injured to the hospitals of Baltimore left the wreckage began to burn," the New York Times reported. Ambulances hurried to the scene, and an express train following the freight provided transportation for those on the other side. Passengers on both trains gave all possible aid to the victims.

Dr. M. L. Bott of Westminster described one wounded passenger who told him, "Doctor, don't bother with me, I am fatally hurt and will die. Go to others whom you can save." Indeed, the man did die a short time later, as the American Sentinel reported. George Stimmel, a laborer from Thurmont, was one of those who was removed from the wreck alive. While aboard the relief train bound for Westminster, he offered "a touching and pathetic prayer for his wife and children, pleading earnestly that they might be supported by almighty God and that the wife might be enabled to train up the children in the paths of Christianity and righteousness," the American Sentinel reported. Rescuers took him to the Hotel Albion in Westminster, where he died the next morning. C. D. Miller, who worked in the Westminster post office and whose legs were crushed in the crash insisted despite his pain on keeping the mail pouches under his head until Charles Thomson, clerk at the post office, arrived and took possession of them.

Clearing the wreckage of the train wreck at Ransom, MD. Photo courtesy of Thurmontimages.com.

About seventy-five men from the Western Maryland and Northern Central railroads used two steam cranes to clear away the wreckage. The *Catoctin Clarion* reported that "With two great steam cranes the three engines were righted and placed upon the tracks, then slowly towed down to the siding near Lawndale. The overturned cars, the broken and twisted axles and machinery were hauled out of the way, and watches, pocketbooks, bank books and other effects belonging to the victims of the wreck were collected."

Burying the dead

The first report to reach Thurmont that same Saturday stated that forty to sixty people had been killed. In fact, twenty-six people died and eleven suffered injuries in what remains the worst accident in the history of the Western Maryland Railway. "The scenes of agony and distress at the homes of dead victims of the accident cannot be described. They were harrowing in the extreme, and those who witnessed them will never forget the wails of widowed women, orphaned children and relatives of the dead," the American Sentinel reported. Yet the loss of life could have been far worse. Though he himself did not survive, reports credit Engineer George Covell of the No. 5 with preventing a larger number of casualties by applying the emergency air brakes as soon as he recognized the danger. Because the track curved at the collision point, "the force of the impact was much less upon the coaches than it would have been in a direct line. Railroad men say it is extremely probable that if the collision had occurred on a straight track the coaches would have been telescoped and the passengers subjected to frightful loss of life."

The towns of Thurmont and Catoctin Furnace suffered the worst—seventeen killed and seven injured, leaving thirteen women widowed and thirty-eight children fatherless, according to the New York Times. "Close family ties and friendships existed among these people. No one was untouched by the tragedy which left a number of widows and fatherless children and dominated thinking in the village of Catoctin Furnace for years," Elizabeth Anderson wrote. Not surprisingly, many of the dead in this small community were related. McClellan Sweeney was the father of Frank and William Sweeney and brother of Harry. Charles Miller and Charles Kelly were brothers-in-law, and E. M. Miller was Charles Miller's son.

E. M. Miller, who escaped injury, helped reporters identify many of the dead and would accept no payment for the service. According to the Carroll County *American Sentinel*, when he had finished, he turned to them and said, "My father, Charles T. Miller, and my uncle, Charles Kelly, are both in the wreck and I am sure they are both dead." He said it with dry eyes, but the newspaper report noted that it was apparent he was "stunned and dazed by the magnitude of the calamity," the American Sentinel reported.

That terrible Saturday night, townspeople gathered at their train station in a macabre replay of a ritual they usually performed every Wednesday, when "Many of the locals would go to the Thurmont station ... and take baskets with good things to eat," Wireman notes. "They sent them down the line to their family who were working on the railroad." The New York Times reported that on this June night, food was far from their thoughts as residents gathered to await word of whether their sons, fathers, and brothers were among the casualties. Some survivors arrived after midnight, bringing more accurate and horrifying accounts. On Sunday, June 18, word spread that train would arrive with the dead at 7:00 p.m. It did not arrive until about 12:30 a.m. Monday, but families waited, as did Clarence Creager and Elmer Black with their hearse:

> During that whole of Sunday great throngs of people were at the station waiting for the train that should bring home the silent disfigured forms of those who had gone forth strong and well. It was about

12:30 a.m. when the first shipment of bodies arrived and then came the long procession of hearses and wagons through the town and in the peaceful moon light wended their way to the Catoctin grief stricken homes where the majority of the dead men lived in life.

Seventeen funerals were held in Thurmont over the next two days. The New York Times reported that out of respect for the town's loss, all of the local businesses closed Monday during the funerals:

Thurmont is an old town and in her long existence has passed through many and varied experiences but never in all her history has she felt such a blow as fell upon her Saturday evening last when the inexpressibly shocking disaster on the WMRR meant so much to her homes and people. Almost three-fourths of the victims of that ill-fated wreck resided in Thurmont and Catoctin; hard-working industrious men, fathers and sons, wage earners and the support, in many instances, of large families.

Because all of the dead worked for the Western Maryland Railway, it quickly became apparent that the company had no relief plan for the victims' families. "If there had been, these unfortunate men would have under that system, provided for their families in case of death," the *Catoctin Clarion* editorialized.

The accident did not tear up track but wreckage had to be removed. According to the Western Maryland Railway Historical Society, Engines No. 41 and 43 were taken to Union Bridge, where they were rebuilt and returned to service. Engine No. 94 was too badly damaged and was scrapped. Engines 41 and 43 were refurbished for about $5,000 each, making the total cost to the railroad company $10,000. The Western Maryland Railway resumed its normal schedule two days after the accident, the same day that families in Thurmont and Catoctin Furnace buried their dead. For the company, business would go on as usual. The American Sentinel reported that authorities in Carroll County were criticized for not holding an inquest after the state's attorney determined it would be an unnecessary procedure; all knew the cause of the accident, and those responsible had been killed in the collision.

Clearing the wreckage of the train wreck at Ransom, MD. Photo courtesy of Thurmontimages.com.

Names of the Dead and Injured, June 17, 1905, Compiled from the American Sentinel, June 23, 1905

- Calvin Brenner, Catoctin Furnace, laborer, killed
- James Brenner, Catoctin Furnace, laborer, killed
- George B. Covell, Hagerstown, engineer on the #5,

killed
- John Crouse, Taneytown, engineer on the #43, killed
- John Davis, Thurmont, laborer, injured
- V. O. Derr, Hagerstown, conductor on the freight train, killed
- Nelson Fraley, Thurmont, laborer, killed
- Peter Frehart, Union Bridge, injured
- Emanuel Fuss, Thurmont, laborer, injured
- Charles Grable, Thurmont, laborer, killed
- James Grushon, Thurmont, laborer, killed
- W. Thomas Hahn, Thurmont, laborer, injured
- Charles Kelly, Thurmont, laborer, killed
- Guy Lynn, Middleburg, laborer, injured
- Edward Martin, Thurmont, laborer, killed
- O. L. Knipple, Hagerstown, fireman on the #41, killed
- Charles Miller, Thurmont, laborer, killed
- Clagett D. Miller, Hagerstown, postal clerk, injured
- Elmer Miller, Thurmont, laborer, killed
- W. H. McNamee, Hagerstown, fireman on the #43, killed
- Daniel Meyers, Highfield, laborer, killed
- L. D. Rice, Hagerstown, engineer on the #41, killed
- John J. St. Leger, Baltimore, fireman on the #5, killed
- E. R. Scott, Hagerstown, substitute fireman, killed
- J. M. Shuff, Catoctin Furnace, killed
- William Shuff, Thurmont, laborer, injured
- Milton Stambaugh, Double Pipe Creek, laborer, injured
- George Stimmel, Thurmont, laborer, killed
- Joseph Stitely, Catoctin Furnace, laborer, killed
- Frank Sweeney, Catoctin Furnace, laborer, killed
- Harry Sweeney, Catoctin Furnace, laborer, killed

- McClellan Sweeney, Catoctin Furnace, laborer, killed
- William Sweeney, Catoctin Furnace, laborer, killed
- Frank Tierney, Hagerstown, laborer, injured
- Clayton Troxell, Rocky Ridge, laborer, injured
- John Whitmore, Thurmont, laborer, injured
- M. Williar[d], Thurmont, laborer, injured
- John Williard, Thurmont, laborer, killed

Accidental Wreck or Sabotage?

T he country was had massive labor problems in 1922. Nationwide, coal miners went on strike beginning April 1 when the United Mine Workers' contract with the coal companies expired on March 31. Around 610,000 miners walked off the job, including over 100,000 miners who weren't with the union.

To make matters worse, it appeared that railroad workers would strike on July 1 because the Railroad Labor Board had announced that it was cutting wages by seven cents an hour, which led the shop workers deciding to strike.

Near the end of the June, Sheriff J. B. Clouse and 10 deputies arrested 105 striking miners near Thomas, W.Va., because they blocked non-striking miners from entering coal mines and doing their jobs.

On June 28, the Western Maryland Railroad provided a train to allow the sheriff and his deputies to transport the miners and their supporters to Parsons, W. Va., where they would have their hearing. The train had 150 people on board, including women and children.

However, something happened along that trip and about 1.5 miles from Hendricks, W. Va., the rear car jumped the tracks, and tumbled down an embankment on Blackwater Grade. The grade drops nearly 4 percent or 1,236 feet as trains travel over 10 miles. The rear car traveled 40 feet down the embankment, crushing the top of the car.

A cloud of dust followed the crash, which didn't seem to bode well. The rest of the train that hadn't derailed halted. People rushed off the train and made their way down the hill to the wreckage. Meanwhile, the remainder of the train headed for help at Hendricks.

The Bluefield Daily Telegraph reported, "As fast as the injured were carried up the steep embankment, they were taken to a nearby farm house which was converted into a temporary hospital, and there given first aid awaiting arrival of the relief train which took them to Parsons and Elkins."

The train reached Hendricks with news of the wreck. Doctors and nurses were hurriedly gathered and along with Judge A. Jay Valentine, who was the judge assigned to the case, boarded a train to head back to the derailment.

Meanwhile, things in Hendricks became unsettled as people accused the striking miners, coal companies, or railroad workers of causing the derailment. The sheriff asked for help from the National Guard, and Co. A 105th MP unit of the West Virginia National Guard was sent to the town to help keep the peace.

Eighty people were injured in the derailment. Although most of the injuries were minor, nine people were listed in serious condition and required admittance to the hospital, and Thomas Konac, a miner from Thomas, was killed. Those with minor injuries who were among the arrested miners were taken from the hospital to the jail where they waited there heading before being sent to Parsons for their hearing before Judge Valentine.

An investigation later listed a broken wheel as the cause for the accident. However, given the state the country was in with a violent, ongoing coal mining strike and an expected railroad strike, the possibility remains, although not proven, that the derailment was caused by sabotage.

During the railroad strike, Western Maryland Railway trains experienced problems from sabotage. Air hoses were cut, switches misapplied and car journals were sanded. Railroad officials reported that there had been hundreds of these incidents in the two months of the strike.

The cut air hoses presented a dangerous problem. The hoses weren't cut all the way through so that they burst when the trains tried to brake. Usually, this meant the car had to be removed from the train and taken onto a sideline where it could be repaired. However, it could also mean that the train couldn't stop, and depending on where it happened, it could be cause an accident.

An Unlucky Train

T hree accidents. Two deaths. One injury. All involved one unlucky Western Maryland Railway train during a single weekend.

The string of unfortunate events began on Saturday, March 13, 1926, at the railmyards in Hagerstown, Maryland. The Western Maryland Railroad arrived in Hagerstown in 1872, and its presence there helped the city grow as the railroad's footprint there grow until it became the busiest point of the Western Maryland Railway system. Not only did nearly all of the Western Maryland Railway trains pass through the city or originate there, other railroad also connected to the Western Maryland Railway at that point. The Jamison Yard was primary rail yard in the city. At railroad's peak, the rail yard could handle 3,000 rail cars.

On March 13, Joseph Mullen, a flagman with the Philadelphia and Reading Railroad, was standing on the rear of the tender of a Philadelphia and Reading engine. The engine was preparing to take a draft of freight cars before continuing on to Harrisburg, Pa.

A Western Maryland Railway engine was also preparing to take freight cars to Baltimore at the same time. It was being run through a cross over track the track the Philadelphia and Reading train was on.

"The tenders sideswiped and Mullen was caught between them and rolled the entire length of the tender," The (Hagerstown) Morning Herald reported.

Mullen was torn apart and crushed. "His head and shoulders were found a distance of twenty feet from his legs and other sections of his body were strewn about the track," according to The Herald Mail.

Police investigated the accident and determined that no inquest was needed. The cause of death was quite obvious. Mullen's remains were shipped to Harrisburg to his widow. He also left behind an orphaned one-year-old child.

That was the first mishap.

A 1954 view of the Hagerstown Rail Yards.

The track was cleared, and the Western Maryland Railway crew continuing with their preparations to take their train to Baltimore. While doing so, T. W. Wilhide, the conductor in charge of the train, dropped a heavy iron bar on his foot. He was injured so badly he had to leave work for the hospital.

That was the second mishap.

Dorsey A. Swink, a local conductor in Hagerstown, was

brought in to relieve Wilhide as the conductor, and the train continued east to Thurmont. On March 14, the train had to shift cars while in Thurmont.

"Swink was attempting to board the engine of the train where he is believed to have missed his footing and fell beneath the wheels of the train," The Herald Mail reported.

His co-workers found him a short time after the accident still alive. They carried Swink on a stretcher for a quarter mile to get to a doctor. Dr. Morris A. Birely rendered first aid, but he was in bad shape. One leg had been severed between the ankle and foot, and the other leg had deep cuts. He also suffered from internal injuries, but he was conscious.

Birely managed to stabilize him, and them sent him on to the Frederick hospital. Swink was still conscious when he reached the hospital, but he died soon after. He was survived by his wife, son, and daughter.

And that was the third mishap.

Three accidents all involving the same Western Maryland Railway train happening over the course of a single weekend. It is fortunate that the train didn't develop a reputation for being jinxed after that.

The Train Derailment
No Passenger Noticed

T he Western Maryland Railway mail train left Hagerstown, Maryland, on time on August 26, 1913, just another day on the daily mail run. However, as it rumbled down the steep grade on Horseshoe Curve on Catoctin Mountain near Sabillasville, Maryland, the driving wheels of the engine left the track.

"The engineer applied the air, but as the drivers on the engine were off the rail, the air was effective only on the five heavy coaches," the Catoctin Clarion reported.

The engine plowed ahead, no longer riding on iron rails but on the railroad ties. The engineers kept applying air to the brakes. Finally, the engineer thought the engine was going to topple into a ravine and jumped. As the coach cars became a greater drag on the engine until the train finally came to a standstill.

"Had the derailed engine skidded a few inches further it would have toppled over and fell into the deep ravine," the Hagerstown Morning Herald reported.

The crew climbed out of the engine to check what had happened. They walked back along the track to locate where the engine had left the rails and to try to figure out what had happened. The track had separated about two inches on the curve, which allowed the engine to leave the rails.

"They found that the train had virtually slid 61 rail lengths, or 2013 feet, and that the flanges on the engine wheels had cut almost all the bolts in the plates which held the rails together," the Catoctin Clarion reported.

Surprisingly, the engine hadn't toppled over. Not all of the engine's wheels had left the track. The pony and trailer wheels had remained on and provided enough guidance to keep the engine upright.

Although the engineer had been injured by jumping from the train, the Catoctin Clarion reported that "passengers scarcely knew anything had happened."

The track remained blocked all night before the engine could be put back on the track.

The railroad's horseshoe bend in Sabillasville, MD. Photo courtesy of Thurmontimages.com

It had not been a good summer for the Western Maryland Railway in Frederick County, Maryland. Although only one person was killed, there had been four accidents that delayed traffic along the railroad.

In late May, a westbound train had passed over the iron bridge west of Thurmont when a refrigerated car loaded with pork jumped the rails and rolled down a 150-foot embankment. Somehow, it was the only one of the 11 cars on the train to derail. The trucks stuck on the side of the embankment, and only the refrigerated car went rolling to the bottom. It remained intact, and the 25 tons of meat were transferred to another rail car and later delivered.

At the end of July, an eastbound train ran into the iron bridge, destroying one of the engine wheels. The engineer applied the brakes and stopped the train before it got out onto the bridge. Although scared, none of the passengers were injured.

A couple of weeks before the August 26 derailment, a flagman fell asleep on the tracks. A westbound train hit him and crushed his leg and back. He died soon after the accident.

The Wreck of the Blue Mountain Express

On June 25, 1915, the Blue Mountain Express bound for Hagerstown, Md., pulled into the Western Maryland Railroad Station in Thurmont about 20 minutes late for its 5:10 p.m. stop in town. Apparently, the train had had a hotbox that needed to be repacked while the train was in Union Bridge, Md., according to Charles Eyler in George Wireman's book, *Gateway to the Mountains.*

In Thurmont, the train hurriedly took on water and dropped off Baltimore's afternoon newspapers for delivery. The stop was short in hopes of making up some lost time.

The express was made up of a Pullman Parlor Car, three coaches, and a baggage car. "Although it was primarily a freight line, the Western Maryland became famous for the excursion trains it ran to the Blue Ridge, and for the Blue Mountain Express, said to have been the finest train in the East," Wireman wrote.

Meanwhile, in Hagerstown, the train dispatcher, Edgar Bloom, was busy trying to keep trains moving along the stretch of track that he watched over. Of the 180 miles under his supervision, all but 20 miles was single track. That meant if two trains were coming from different directions, he had to notify the nearest station to have one train pull off onto a siding until the other train passed.

Bloom had been doing this for a while and knew his job, but today, he was having trouble communicating to the east. A storm earlier in the week had knocked down a telegraph line. Add to that, the general confusion of a hectic day and Bloom lost track of countermanding an order that gave the Blue Mountain Express the right of way, according to the Adams County News.

From Thurmont, the next stop was Sabillasville, Md. Outside of Thurmont, the Blue Mountain Express started up the mountain on a section of single track that ran for just over two miles.

Around 5:30 p.m., local residents heard the familiar sound of the Blue Mountain Express's train whistle, but instead of stopping, it continued blowing. People knew something was the matter and rushed to where they heard the whistle.

On the tracks, it's not certain how soon the engineers saw the trouble coming at them. The eastbound Baltimore Unlimited came head to head with the westbound Blue Mountain Express.

"It is presumed that the engineers of both trains believed the other had been ordered to take the siding to allow his train to pass.", all-steel cars helped minimize loss of life," the Adams County News reported.

The two engines hit. The impact crumpled some cars and knocked others off the High Bridge over Owens Creek into the ravine 100 feet below.

Seconds before the crash, Fireman Vendergerst on the Baltimore Unlimited "made a thrilling leap for safety," according to the Frederick News. It did him little good. He was found later with a broken back and legs broken in several places. He was taken to the hospital in Hagerstown.

R. B. Taylor of Westminster, Md., was sitting in the smoking car when he felt the train slowing. He thought the engineer might be applying the emergency brake.

"I thrust my head out of the window and beheld a terrifying sight," Taylor told the Hagerstown Herald-Mail. "The engine and tender of the Blue Mountain was over the bridge, while the baggage car was smashed in, part of it falling into the ravine behind the engine and tender."

Uninjured, Taylor grabbed his things and headed for the door along with the other passengers in the car.

He was one of the lucky ones.

The Blue Mountain Express on High Bridges on June 24, 1915. Only the eastbound engine is visible. The westbound engine had already been removed by this time. Photo courtesy of Thurmontimages.com.

Thomas B. South of Hagerstown was in the passenger car next to the baggage car that crashed into the ravine. He felt a "grating sensation before the crash came." The impact threw him forward against the seat in front of him.

"Mr. South said he could feel the car in which he was riding turn almost completely around and that it then tilted, as if it was going into the ravine," reported the Hagerstown Herald-Mail. "Women screamed and children cried when the awful compact came, and great difficulty was experienced in getting them out of the cars."

Harry Smith of Hagerstown was seated in a passenger car of the Blue Mountain Express and "he felt the car topple and pieces of glass flew in every direction and many persons were badly cut," according to the *Hagerstown Herald-Mail*.

The two trains hit head-on. The baggage car on the Blue Mountain Express fell into the ravine, carrying with it two passengers, Mrs. W. C. Chipchase and her son, Walter.

"Mrs. Chipchase was going to be admitted to a sanitarium, was reclining in a baggage car, son and nurse with her, the nurse left to stroll through the train, which probably saved her," the Adams County News reported.

Mrs. Chipchase died in the fall, but Walter was found unconscious and groaning when rescuers reached him.

The Frederick News reported that Walter was taken to a cottage at Blue Ridge Summit, Pa., where his sister Ethel had been waiting for her brother and mother to arrive. He died around midnight.

The engines of the two trains had locked together on impact, "appearing as almost one engine to the horrified rescuers who quickly gathered on the scene. Had the engines ricocheted off of one another, there undoubtedly would have been more causalities," according to a historical study of Catoctin National Park.

Wireman wrote, "Coals were falling from one of the boilers and for a time threatened to set fire to the wooden structure of the bridge. The whistle on one of the engines had stuck in an open position and kept blowing until all of the steam was gone."

Within minutes of the crash, about 100 people had gathered to help the survivors and find the dead amid the debris.

As the passengers and crew were located and pulled from the wreckage, two bodies were seen that could not be reached easily. Fireman Hayes' body was hanging from the train's cab, but no one could reach it because the cab was hung over the ravine.

"It was impossible to move the body for fear that the slightest motion would hurl it to the bottom of the ravine nearly 100 feet below," the *Frederick News* reported.

Dr. Morris Birely of Thurmont was the first doctor on the scene. He went to work treating the wounded as best he could. He worked into the night using gas lanterns for light.

The Western Maryland Railroad sent two special trains to help in transporting the dead and wounded from the area. One train came from the east and the other the west.

All of the wreckage except the connected locomotives had been cleared from the bridge by morning.

"People were still wondering the next day how the two engines had stayed on the rails. But it was easy to see how the wreck had occurred. The bridge is 'blind' from both directions. From the east, a train passes out of a deep, curving cut right onto the bridge. From the west, an engineer had a little more visibility but was also on a curve and was traveling down-hill, making a quick stop impossible," Wireman wrote.

In the end, six died in the crash of the Blue Mountain Express. They were: Coleman Cook, engineer; Luther Hull, fireman; J. R. Hayes, fireman; Mrs. W. C. Chipchase, Baltimore; Walter Chipchase, Baltimore. Twelve others suffered severe injuries. An investigation revealed that a mix-up in the all-important right-of-way orders issued from Hagerstown had caused the crash.

Bloom "Pale and worn, the unmistakable signs of the worry he has experienced since hearing the result of his mistake," according to the Adams County News, accepted responsibility for the accident.

Oddly, there were three Western Maryland Railroad officials on the Blue Mountain Express on their way to a meeting about preventing wrecks.

The wreck of the Blue Mountain Express on June 24, 1915. This picture was altered at some point to make it appear as if the engines are touching. You can see that part of the photograph has been cut out. Photo courtesy of Thurmontimages.com.

Did One Death Lead to Six?

What if there was another contributing factor in the accident no one realized because it had happened months earlier?

William H. Webb was a 65-year-old watchman on the bridges west of Thurmont. Each day, he would walk to his shanty next to the bridges from his home on Kelbaugh Road. Every day, his wife, Sarah, would have one of their children or grandchildren take William his lunch.

"As watchman of those bridges, Mr. Webb's position was an important one. The safety of many passengers and trains depended upon his watchfulness during the hours of the night. He walked those bridges at regular intervals during all hours of the night," the *Frederick Post* reported.

William H. Webb, the man who might have been able to prevent the wreck of the Blue Mountain Express. Photo courtesy of Roger Troxell.

By 1915, he'd been an employee of the Western Maryland Railroad for 35 years. His job was isolated, but he enjoyed it.

Webb was Roger Troxell's great-grandfather. According to stories that his mother told him, "One of the children or grandchildren took him his lunch one day. It was pouring down rain and he found him (Webb) sitting on the railing holding his umbrella, and he was dead."

This differs from the accounts in the Frederick Post and Catoctin Clarion. They reported that the day watchman had found William lying beside the cross-tie block on February 24, 1915.

"When found his overcoat was drawn up over his shoulders, and a raised umbrella lay beside him," the *Frederick Post* reported.

The *Catoctin Clarion* explained that it appeared as if Webb had come east from his shack across the iron bridge to "signal" the Fast Mail train going west soon after 6 o'clock, and while walking to his post east of the bridge was stricken with heart trouble and died.

The day watchman telephoned to Thurmont, and Dr. Birely and Magistrate E. E. Black came out to the bridges to examine the body. No marks were found on it, and Birely said that heart failure was the cause of death.

Although this was months before the summer wreck of the Blue Mountain Express, there's no indication that another watchman was hired to replace Webb. Also, one of the trains that wrecked was the fast mail train that Webb usually signaled.

Had Webb still been alive and on the job, he may have been able to signal the trains to stop before they wrecked on the bridges. Bloom may also have been able to call the shanty directly about the mix-up rather than telegraphing a message to the Western Maryland Railroad Station in Thurmont and hope to stop the train before it left the station.

LABOR ISSUES

Labor Troubles on the Railroad

It was an accident waiting to happen; one that some people were probably hoping would happen because it might get them a larger salary.

The country was entering the fifth month of a nationwide railroad strike in August 1922. The Railroad Labor Board had announced that it was cutting wages by seven cents an hour (about $1.35 an hour today), which led the shop workers to strike, though they were the only railroad work group that did so. Still, there were 400,000 shop workers on strike, including 1,400 who worked for the Baltimore and Ohio Railroad and the Western Maryland Railway in Cumberland, Md.

It was the largest railroad work stoppage since 1894, and it became a bitter one. The railroad companies brought in 300,000 strikebreakers to fill the vacant positions. Violence began escalating so that by the end of July, the National Guard was on duty in seven states and 2,200 deputy U.S. marshals were carefully watching meetings and picket lines.

When a proposed settlement by President Warren G. Harding failed, people began to realize that the strike might last for some time.

During the strike, Western Maryland Railway trains began experiencing problems. Air hoses were cut, switches misapplied and car journals were sanded. Railroad officials reported that there had been hundreds of these incidents in the two months of the strike.

The cut air hoses presented a dangerous problem. The hoses weren't cut all the way through so that they burst when the trains tried to brake. Usually this meant the car had to be removed from the train and taken onto a sideline where it could be repaired.

"It is possible that a serious derailment might have occurred from these sources, causing loss of life of passengers and crew," reported the *Cumberland Evening Times*.

In one instance, the Al G. Barnes circus train had its journals sanded and hoses cut, but the sabotage was discovered before the train left Cumberland. Even so, the train was unable to leave the city before the repairs could be made putting the circus well behind in its touring schedule that season.

The Western Maryland Railway hired the Burns Detective Agency to find out what was going on. The detectives began investigating and managed to take photographs of employees sabotaging the trains without them knowing it. Railroad officials identified the employees. Some were striking shop men, but others were from other departments and had been with the Western Maryland Railway for years.

The men were shown the pictures during their disciplinary hearings right before they were fired.

Despite the convictions, the Western Maryland Railway was still be on the alert for sabotage. "Every freight and passenger train is carefully guarded from such criminal acts as far as possible, it was stated, before they are dispatched from terminals now," the newspaper reported.

The strike continued until September when an agreement was reached. At that time, strikebreakers began resigning their positions at the B&O Railroad hired back its shop men. In some instances in South Cumberland, strikebreakers "were stoned, and chased and struck with dinner-buckets and forced to run in various directions. Several resented this and free-for-all fights occurred, including a dog fight, in the street during the fracas. Several of them were badly bruised and beaten," reported the *Cumberland Evening Times* on September 19, 1922.

The Western Maryland Railway was more reticent, in part, perhaps from the amount of loss that the railway incurred because of the sabotage.

One of the many employees of the Western Maryland Railway. Photo courtesy of Wikimedia Commons.

Bridge Go Boom

Around 10 a.m. on September 15, 1922, citizens in Cumberland, Maryland, were hard at work when a loud explosion shook the windows in homes and buildings. Some of them actually broke or cracked.

People ran into the streets, looking around for the source of the explosion.

Word soon spread that someone had tried to blow up the Western Maryland Railroad bridge over the Potomac River. It connected the Welton Tunnel with South Cumberland.

"There is evidence that 20 sticks of dynamite were used, inducing a detonation which roused the entire South End and was heard over the city," the Cumberland Evening Times reported.

People might not have known who the actual culprits were, but they knew they were railroaders.

The country was in the sixth month of a nationwide railroad strike. The Railroad Labor Board had announced that it was cutting wages by 7 cents an hour (about $1.35 an hour today), which led the shop workers to strike, though they were the only railroad work group that did so. Still, there were 400,000 shop workers on strike, including 1,400 who worked for the Baltimore and Ohio Railroad and the Western Maryland Railway in Cumberland.

Acts of violence, including blowing up railroad bridges across the country, marked the strike. Western Maryland Railroad trains had experienced problems throughout the strike. Air hoses were cut, switches misapplied and car journals (part of the axle assembly) were sanded. Railroad officials reported that there had been hundreds of these incidents during the strike.

The explosion had been set off on the West Virginia side of the bridge. The explosion had damaged the bridge, but not significantly. The abutment had cracked, a girder had sheared off, and rails had been loosened. Damage was estimated at $500 (about $9,500 today).

An aerial view of the Welton Tunnel near Cumberland, MD. Photo courtesy of the Library of Congress.

Inspectors and repairmen were quickly brought in, and rail traffic was allowed to continue. Guards protected them from attack while they repaired and inspected the tracks.

"The fact that no one was hurt and the bridge was not destroyed nor transportation seriously interfered with, is not due to any lack of destructive and murderous intent and effort on the part of the perpetrator or perpetrators of the evil deed," the Cumberland Evening Times reported.

The source of the dynamite was believed to be the Cumberland Cement Company at Ackerman, 10 miles south of Cumberland. Days earlier, company personnel had reported that "76 sticks of high-powered dynamite" had been stolen. This worried people that another explosion might be set off with the remaining dynamite, although this didn't happen.

The bridge was a strategic one for rail traffic. Had it been destroyed, it would have disrupted much of the coal traffic from Western Maryland. Trains would have had to detour over the Baltimore and Ohio rail lines to Baird, W. Va.

The strike was the largest railroad work stoppage since 1894. According to archival material, the railroad companies brought in 300,000 strikebreakers to fill the vacant positions, and violence had escalated quickly. This led to the National Guard being called up in seven states and 2,200 deputy U.S. marshals to keep rail traffic moving.

THE WAR BETWEEN THE STATES

Lincoln's Last Train Ride

On April 21, 1865, a locomotive slowly pulled out of the depot in Washington D.C. carrying about 300 people. Those who saw the train generally bowed their heads. Many of them cried. The train was carrying the remains of President Abraham Lincoln who had been assassinated a week earlier and his son, Willie Lincoln. John Wilkes Booth has assassinated Lincoln earlier in the month, and Willie had died in 1862. They were returning home to Springfield, IL.

The Lincoln Special

The train consisted of the funeral car, baggage cars and coaches, and the engine. A photo of Lincoln was mounted on the front of the train over the cowcatcher. The funeral car was decorated with black garland and silver tassels and had a U.S. coat of arms painted on the side of it.

"With sixteen wheels for a smoother ride, rounded monitor ends, fine woodwork, upholstered walls, [and] etched glass windows" this funeral car surely was a sight to behold," Scott Trostel wrote in *The Lincoln Funeral Train: The Final Journey and National Funeral for Abraham Lincoln.*

The journey would essentially retrace Lincoln's trip as President-elect from Illinois to Washington in reverse. The only change was that it deleted a stop in Pittsburgh and added one in Chicago. Although it did not travel along the Western Maryland Railroad, it did travel on rail lines that eventually became part of the Western Maryland Railway.

Lincoln's funeral train waiting on the tracks in Harrisburg, PA. Photo courtesy of the Library of Congress.

Coming to Harrisburg

The first stop on the journey had been in Baltimore. From there, the train headed to Harrisburg, PA, Gov. Andrew Curtin and a delegation from Pennsylvania met the train at the state line just south of Shrewsbury, PA. They joined the Maryland delegation in the front car and rode to Harrisburg allowing for a short stop in York, PA.

The train arrived in the capital city amid a hard rain around 8:30 p.m. on Friday, April 21. As it passed the west end of the Northern Central Railway bridge, a cannon fired and church bells pealed across the city.

The train halted only when the funeral car sat on Market Street. The heavy rain was joined by thunder and lightning as members of the Veterans Corps carried the coffin from the coach to a hearse that had been specially made by Harrisburg undertakers, W. W. Boyer and Peter R. Boyd, for the occasion.

Four white horses then pulled the hearse down Market Street to the square, north on Second Street to State Street, and then up State Street to the capital building. The procession that followed the hearse was led by Col. Henry McCormick and included city ministers, Mayor Augustus Roumfort and some of the city's leading citizens. A band playing a funeral dirge led the next group of mourners that included Gov. Curtin, his staff, state officials, another band, two regiments of Pennsylvania soldiers and one unit of New York soldiers.

The railroad car that carried President Abraham Lincoln's body from Washington to Illinois. Courtesy of the Library of Congress.

"The entire procession was lit by the city's new chemical streetlights, which gave off a deep orange glow," George F. Nagle wrote in *The Bugle*, the Camp Curtin Historical Society newsletter.

At the capital, the President's coffin was placed in a catafalque in the House of Representatives chamber. The catafalque was made from lots of black cloth placed over the clerk's desk and speaker's dais so that neither could be seen.

Paying Respects

A public viewing began at 9:30 p.m. and for two and a half hours, an estimated 10,000 mourners waited in the storm outside the capital for an opportunity to pay their last respects to the man who had lead the country through the Civil War.

They entered the chamber in two lines. The lines separated at the foot of the coffin so that a line filed along either side of the coffin to view the President's body.

"Each line exited through specially rigged doorways through the large windows on opposite sides of the chamber. So many filed through that the undertaker had to re-chalk the visibly discoloring face and dust the body before the chamber could be reopened the next morning," Nagle wrote.

Another public viewing began on Saturday morning at 7 a.m. and ran until 9 a.m. The doors to the chamber were then closed and the funeral procession reformed to take the President's coffin back to the funeral train.

At 8:30 a.m., church bells began tolling and cannons were fired to notify the city to prepare for the funeral procession. An estimated 40,000 people lined the streets of Harrisburg along the route and waited for the procession to pass. This was roughly twice as many people than lived in the city at the time.

Once the procession passed, many of the mourners followed behind to accompany the procession back to the train.

The Journey Continues

The funeral train pulled out of the Harrisburg depot at 11:15 a.m. heading for Philadelphia. As the train left the city, it passed a large American flag that had been spread across a field where it could be seen from the train. Crowds of people stood on either side of the flag and removed their hats as the train passed, according to the *New York Herald*.

The journey to Lincoln's final resting place would take two weeks and pass through Washington, Maryland, Pennsylvania, New York, Ohio, Indiana, and Illinois.

The engine of the Lincoln funeral train. Photo courtesy of the Library of Congress.

The Gettysburg Telegraph Girl

When the Confederate Army entered Gettysburg, Pa., from the west on July 1, 1863, people were in a panic. Some fled. Some hid in their basements. Many watched through windows, peeking around curtains, hoping the soldiers and fighting would pass them by. They expected lots of fighting in the streets and that the army would take any food and supplies they needed.

The army also sought to secure their position in the town, trying to halt the trains and take over the telegraph communications. They were in enemy territory and wanted to slow any calls for help for the Union troops as much as possible.

The Gettysburg Railroad operated along 17 miles from 1858 to 1870. It ran from Gettysburg to Hanover Junction. The Gettysburg Railroad Station also served as a local telegraph office.

Train stations used telegraphs to alert each other about the movement of trains in order to avoid accidents on the line. It was a relatively new technology during the Civil War that proved itself under fire. The telegraph key interrupts an electrical circuit. The telegrapher taps out short and long interruptions-dots and dashes-to send messages in Morse Code. The messages travelled along wires strung on poles, usually along railroad rights of way. However, from the train stations, additional lines and poles could be strung to other locations. Each location needed a telegraph key that would be wired into the telegraph lines and a telegrapher who knew how to use the key and understood Morse Code.

As the Confederate Army sought to secure the town, an

unknown young girl at the station had the presence of mind to realize that the soldiers would either commandeer the telegraph to try to send messages south or destroy it so the Union Army couldn't use it.

She disconnected the equipment from the telegraph wires and carried it to Cemetery Hill, nearly three-quarters of a mile away. Although young, she remained calm as she walked through the town as it filled with enemy soldiers, some of whom were probably looking for what she had hidden in her basket. Her youth and gender helped her in this regard because the soldiers would not expect the telegrapher to be a young woman. Even the Union soldiers under the command of Maj. General Oliver O. Howard were probably surprised to learn the young woman was a telegrapher.

She changed their opinions, though. "Placing it upon a black of wood, she instructed the boys how to cut the line and reconnect the wires, and seated upon the ground sent and received news for the officers all through the battle," the Washington Daily Reporter reported in 1890.

She was needed on the scene because few, if any, of the soldiers would have known Morse Code.

Fighting took place on the hill all three days of the battle. It was where the Union Army dug in after the Confedcrates drove them out of Gettysburg on the first day. The Union then had to defend that position from repeated attacks and shelling from Confederate troops both inside and outside of the town.

The young telegrapher remained there through it all. She didn't even flee when a man just six feet from her was struck and killed by a shell. She supported the Union cause and did what she could to help.

When the fighting ended, she disconnected the system and took it back to the station.

Her name, sadly, has been lost to history. It is believed

that she was the adopted daughter or Mr. Lee, perhaps Brown Lee, in Washington County, Pa., which is far from Gettysburg on the west end of the state.

This story was written by Mary Dye in 1890. She said it was older to her by Capt. O. R. McNary who knew the girl because he was near her temporary office during the battle. The story was published in newspapers across the country as more information was sought about the courageous telegraph girl.

The Gettysburg Railroad Station, which became part of the Western Maryland Railroad. Photo courtesy of the Library of Congress.

A variation on this story says the girl was a female schoolteacher from Waynesboro, Pa., who became the chief telegrapher at Gettysburg. Her name was Samantha French, and her story is part of an entry about female telegraphers in

Library of Congress Civil War Desk Reference and in an article titled "Waynesboro in the Civil War." She also would have been about 28 at the time of the battle.

Although the story has some of the details wrong, such as the distance between the station and Cemetery Hill, and others have been disputed by modern historians, the story has made it into the history books. In fact, although her name was not known, she was included as a mini-figure in a Lego Ideas set of the Lincoln Train Station. It included three figures: Abraham Lincoln, the stationmaster, and a girl holding a telegraph key.

Capt. Oliver R. McNary. Photo courtesy of Wikimedia Commons.

The Gettysburg Railroad was the railroad President Abraham Lincoln would travel upon to reach Gettysburg on

November 18 when he arrived to deliver his famous Gettysburg Address the following day to consecrate Soldiers' National Cemetery.

Although not originally part of the Western Maryland Railway system, it did become so in 1917 through a number of mergers. The Susquehanna, Gettysburg & Potomac Railway took over the tracks in 1870. It then became part of the Hanover Junction, Hanover and Gettysburg Railroad in 1874, the Baltimore and Harrisburg Railway in 1886, and the Western Maryland Railway in 1917.

The Government Takes Control

T he U.S. government is not above being heavy handed when it needs something. This was especially apparent during the Civil War. Near the beginning of the war, President Abraham Lincoln needed to ensure Maryland remained in the Union so Washington D. C. would not be surrounded by Confederate States. This likely would have ended the war quickly in favor of the South.

Although Maryland hadn't voted on secession in early 1861, it was waving red flags indicating the legislature might be leaning in that direction. Efforts were made to hinder if not stop the passage of federal troops through Baltimore. "While Hicks was pro-Union, he authorized Maryland militia to prevent the passage of more Union troop trains by disabling railroad bridges and cutting telegraph wires," Dennis Keating wrote in an article on the Cleveland Civil War Roundtable website.

Actions like this led Lincoln to say, "Union soldiers are neither birds to fly over Maryland nor moles to burrow under it."

He went further and invoked Article I, Section 9, Clause 2 of the U.S. Constitution which states, "The Privilege of Writ of Habeas Corpus shall not be suspended, unless when in Cases of Rebellion or Invasion the public Safety may require it."

With states in rebellion and Congress not in session, Lincoln authorized Commander of the Army Winfield Scott to suspend Habeas Corpus if necessary to ensure the safety of the military supply lines between Philadelphia and Washington.

The president went even further and began having the military arrest Confederate sympathizers in the Maryland Legislature and other pro-South politicians to make sure Maryland would fail and the state would stay in the Union.

The federal overreach continued into the war after the largest and deadliest battle of the Civil War was fought at Gettysburg, Pennsylvania, during July 1-3, 1863.

According to the Western Maryland Railroad annual report for the year ending September 30, 1863, following the battle, "Immediately after the Battle of Gettysburg, the road and rolling stock were for about eight days under the control of the Government. No passengers or freight, other than for the use of the Army, were transported over the road. Our entire equipment was at the service of the Government, and we have no hesitation in saying, has done them valuable service."

It began with the government using the trains to transport needed supplies to the troops at Gettysburg. With the government in control of the rail line, Western Maryland trains could be sent anywhere over any existing rail line.

However, Gen. Herman Haupt, Commander of the U.S. Military Railroads, was not impressed by the Western Maryland Railroad lines. After he visited the Relay House, north of Baltimore, he wrote in his memoirs, "I found the Western Maryland Railroad entirely without equipment or facilities for the business to be thrown immediately upon it. It had not experienced officers, no water stations, sidings or turntables, or wood for a business exceeding three or four trains per day, while the necessities of the service required thirty trains per day to be passed over it."

Following the immediate need for supplies, U.S. Quartermaster General Montgomery Meigs sent a construction train to Westminster, Maryland, to build sidings and other needed infrastructure to turn the city into a supply depot. This shortened the trips along the rail lines, allowing for supplies to be delivered to where they were needed quicker.

A lot more trains started running over the lines as well. General Haupt wrote to Gen. Rufus Ingalls, Chief Quartermaster of the Army of the Potomac, "It will be all-important, on the arrival of a convey, to unload each and every car on the main v track and send back immediately. This duty will require the most efficient officer of your staff. The rapidity with which cars can be unloaded will measure the capacity of this road to supply the army."

It was all very confusing but Haupt was a skilled logistician. He delegated duties and quickly got things under control and moving relatively smoothly.

Because of the increased traffic on the railroad, there was a greater chance of accidents. A large line like the Baltimore and Ohio had telegraph lines along the right of way that allowed stationmasters to communicate. The Western Maryland Railroad didn't have this, so mounted couriers were used, carrying messages to and from the stations to avoid train accidents.

While the Federal control hindered the ability of the Western Maryland Railroad to make money, it did provide some protection. Confederate troops were known to attack trains and destroy rail lines. While the Federal government was in control, it added armed escorts to the trains.

Trains were also used to move troops to the front lines and the wounded, the dead, and prisoners from the front lines.

Something similar to this happened during World War I when the Federal Government, through the Director General of Railroads took control of the U.S. railway system from December 27, 1917, through February 28, 1920.

Mr. Lincoln Goes to Gettysburg

The Gettysburg Address in all its brevity is considered one of the most important pieces of American writing ever penned.

President Abraham Lincoln delivered the speech at the dedication of Soldiers' National Cemetery on November 19, 1863, just four months after the Battle of Gettysburg. Although his brief remarks are the ones remembered from that day, he was not the featured speaker. Former U.S. Secretary of State Edward Everett spoke for nearly two hours that day as people stood in the sun listening. Lincoln, on the other hand, spoke for about two minutes.

The Constitution Center said of the speech, "In his powerful address, Lincoln embraced the Declaration of Independence, recalling how the nation was 'conceived in Liberty, and dedicated to the proposition that all men are created equal.' By resurrecting these promises, Lincoln committed post-Civil War America to 'a new birth of freedom.' Following the Civil War, the Reconstruction Amendments—the Thirteenth, Fourteenth, and Fifteenth Amendments—abolished slavery, wrote the Declaration of Independence's commitment to freedom and equality into the Constitution, and promised to ban racial discrimination in voting. In so doing, the amendments sought to make Lincoln's "new birth of freedom" a constitutional reality."

For all its importance in U.S. history, the Gettysburg Address almost wasn't written. The committee putting together the dedication of the new Soldiers' National Cemetery sent out hundreds of invitations to state and federal politicians in

Union states in preparation for the dedication in Gettysburg.

When they received back President Lincoln's acceptance, they were unsure what to do. Some of them had heard him speak. "They were familiar with his political talks and debates but many questioned his ability to say the right things on such a solemn occasion," Harold A. Williams wrote in the *Western Maryland Railway Story*.

About two weeks before the dedication, David Wills, a committee member, wrote the president, saying, "It is the desire that, after the Oration, you, as Chief Executive of the nation, formally set apart these grounds to their sacred use by a few appropriate remarks."

The arrangements were made, and at noon on November 18, 1863, a special four-car train decorated with flags and red, white, and blue bunting pulled out of Washington, D. C. along the Baltimore and Ohio Railroad. Besides Lincoln, the passengers included Secretary of State William Seward, Secretary of the Interior John Usher, Postmaster General Montgomery Blair, several foreign officials, Lincoln's secretary John Nicolay, and Lincoln's assistant secretary, John Hay.

A section of the last car had a drawing room partitioned off, which is where Lincoln stayed. The weight of commanding a nation at war weighed heavily on him. Henry Clay Cochrane, a Marine lieutenant who stayed near Lincoln during the trip, said the President "was looking sallow, sunken-eyed, thin, care-worm, and very quiet." Cochrane said at one point it was nice to see the President chuckle over the inaccurate speculations the newspapers were making about troop actions.

Those aboard the train must have also wondered about how the President would be received in Baltimore. When he had last been through the city, more than two prior, it had been under cover of darkness in order to thwart a plot to assassinate the president-elect on his way to his inauguration.

The train arrived at Camden Station at 1:20 p.m. and was met by a crowd of around 200 people that included B&O Railroad President John W. Garrett, B&O Railroad Superintendent William Prescott Smith, and Northern Central Railroad President J. D. Cameron. To the surprise of some, the crowd actually cheered the President.

President Lincoln delivers the Gettysburg Address. Courtesy of Wikimedia Commons.

The cars were then separated and drawn by horses along Howard and Cathedral streets to the Bolton Street station. The President stepped out onto his the rear platform of his car and waved to the crowd several times during the transfer.

At the Bolton Street Station, the train was reassembled and an additional car added. William E. Barton wrote in Lincoln at Gettysburg, "When the train was made up again a baggage car was added, fitted up as a dining car for those members of the party who had left Washington without lunch, which number included the President."

The train then left along what would become part of the Western Maryland Railroad at 2 p.m. The positive and enthusiastic receptions seems to have bolstered the President's spirits.

The train used the Hanover Brach Railroad and the Gettysburg Railroad to reach Gettysburg.

It is known that Lincoln hadn't completed his speech by the time he left for Gettysburg. He had told a correspondent days before the dedication that the speech was written "but not finished."

Many people believe that Lincoln made edits to his speech while on the Western Maryland Railroad train. This is not to say he wrote the speech on the train, but it would not have been out of place to review what he had written. At the very least, he would have pondered over his speech. Williams wrote, "Lincoln must have worked over the speech in his mind as the train moved toward Gettysburg." The trip was long and knowing he had remarks to give, it would not have been unusual for him to review his remarks and make any needed changes.

Williams wrote of something else that happened on the trip, "[W]hen the trip was over, Lincoln approached Conductor Eckert, talked to him a while, and, with the words: Here's something for you. Take it. May God be with you." Then he gave Eckert a large silver watch that the conductor treasured and kept safe in a bank box in Baltimore.

The railroad also has another connection to Lincoln in the Gettysburg Address because David Wills, who was secretary for the Western Maryland Railroad, hosted the President in his home the night of November 18. J. G. Randall wrote in Lincoln the President, Springfield to Gettysburg, that while staying in the Wills House, "the President probably worked over his first draft, then made his 'second draft' … which is almost certainly that which Lincoln held in his hand when he delivered the Address."

The President delivered the address on November 19, and at the time, few recognized it as significant, in part, because of its brevity. Over the years, as people have pondered those carefully chosen words, they have come to realize how much it says about America and our purpose. It is taught in schools. Other speakers have used phrases from it to add gravitas to their speeches. Other countries have incorporated its phrases and sentiments into their Constitution.

The Gettysburg Address is the most important speech in American history and the Western Maryland Railroad played a part in making it happen.

Railroad Operations

The End of Rocky Ridge

Rocky Ridge, Md., disappeared in 1913. "So far as railroad matters are concerned Rocky Ridge does not exist and hereafter that station will be known as Emmitsburg Junction," the Catoctin Clarion reported.

The Western Maryland Railroad station at Rocky Ridge, Md., had opened in Rocky Ridge in 1870 with Sheridan Biggs serving as the first freight agent and telegraph operator. He served in that position until 1907. Over the years, he had had to deal with confusion over passengers knowing that they needed to switch trains at Rocky Ridge in order to get to Emmitsburg, Md., on the Emmitsburg Railroad. They would leave the Western Maryland Railroad train and board a small train made up of an engine, baggage car, smoker/mail car, and parlor car owned by the Emmitsburg Railroad.

Though only a few miles long, the railroad was well run. The Adams County News noted in 1916, "…there is to-day a short distance from Gettysburg a railroad planned, built and financed through the efforts of women, a road which was built some 40 years ago and which to-day untroubled by strikes and other unpleasantness, is paying steadily 4 per cent on the original investment."

The Daughters of Charity owned 70 percent of the stock in the railroad, according to the Adams County News. This is not surprising since one of the stops on the line was at St. Joseph College. Students traveling to Mount St. Mary's College also used the railroad to get to and from school.

"It is probably the only road in existence where the possession of an ordinary ticket entitles one to parlor-car accommodations," the Adams County News reported.

But something about the switching location confused passengers, despite the conductor often calling out, "Rocky Ridge, change for Emmitsburg."

The Rocky Ridge station on the Western Maryland Railway. Photo courtesy of the Western Maryland Railway Historical Society.

A.V.D. Watterson, Esq., a Pittsburgh attorney and president of the Mount St. Mary's Alumni Association, lobbied to the Western Maryland Railroad for years to change the name of Rocky Ridge to Emmitsburg Junction to make it clearer that the station was a changing point for passengers.

In 1913, he wrote the directors of the Western Maryland Railroad directors again. This time, he noted in his letter, "Since a through line is now established from Pittsburgh to Baltimore, which will permit of persons going through to Emmitsburg with only one change of cars, it is important to your Company to make a change of this kind, and I, therefore, again call your attention to it."

This time, the directors agreed with his reasoning and renamed Rocky Ridge Emmitsburg Junction on all of its documentation and schedules. However, the post office remained Rocky Ridge, so anything being mailed to Emmitsburg Junction had to be sent to Rocky Ridge, which was also confusing, just not for the railroad passengers.

The Clarion noted that the change might have come too late because Thurmont might soon become the transfer point for rail travelers if the Frederick and Hagerstown Railway continued to grow.

The same train station as Rocky Ridge, but from a different angle, and now the sign reads, "Emmitsburg Junction." Photo courtesy of the Western Maryland Railway Historical Society.

"It is hoped a trolley road will soon be built from Thurmont to Mt. St. Mary's for the benefit and convenience of the hundreds of students attending college at that place, and also for the benefit of the many people residing between these two points," the newspaper reported.

This did not happen, but with the growth of automobile

travel, so few people were using the Emmitsburg Railroad by 1935 that it became freight only. It ceased operation in 1940.

Even then, not all the stations along the Western Maryland Railway line were alerted to the change.

In 1959, Mrs. James Tucker and her daughter, both from Boston, traveled to New York City where they purchased a ticket to Emmitsburg via Emmitsburg Junction. They boarded the train for the five-hour trip to St. Joseph College.

When the New Englanders arrived at Emmitsburg Junction, they found a worn out railway station but no railroad, not even a track," the Gettysburg Times reported.

Luckily, they met Guy Baker who was driving a mail and express truck. He offered to take the ladies to the college.

Emmitsburg Junction still continues to pop up on modern maps from time to time, although it should have ceased to exist along the railroad. A 1992 Frederick County trash map showed Emmitsburg Junction as north of MD 77 while Rocky Ridge was south of the highway. Even today, if you type Emmitsburg Junction into Mapquest, it will take you to Rocky Ridge.

The Old Switcheroo

The driving idea behind railroads as a preferred mode of transportation was convenience, speed, and efficiency. Things didn't always work out that way, though.

In the mid- to late-1800s, both the Western Maryland Railroad and the Baltimore and Ohio Railroad operated out of Baltimore. Both had separate stations. The Western Maryland Railroad ended at Hillen Station, near Hillen Street and North Avenue, on the northeastern edge of downtown Baltimore. The B&O Railroad used Camden Station, located near Camden and Howard Streets. The two stations were over two miles apart, with no connecting rail line between them for passengers who needed to change trains.

In later years, passengers could switch trains at the same station. They would deboard one train and board another on a different track at the same station. However, during the 19th century, passengers transferring between the Western Maryland and the B&O had to take a horse-drawn streetcar, hire a hackney cab or horse-drawn carriage, or walk the two miles if they had time and means.

It was anything but convenient or efficient.

As for the passenger's baggage, either the passengers could carry it themselves or it could be transferred using an express service or freight wagon, depending on the railroad's arrangements with local delivery services.

It also didn't matter how important you were; if you were traveling on the Western Maryland and B&O, you had to bridge the gap between the two stations in Baltimore. That gap also came close to causing a change in the course of

American history.

When Abraham Lincoln traveled from Springfield, Ill., to Washington, D.C., for his first presidential inauguration in 1861, that two-mile gap came close to ending his life. The country was on the verge of the Civil War, and Lincoln's election had pushed the southern states closer to secession.

Abraham Lincoln arriving in Washington the 1861 inauguration after avoiding an assassination plot in Baltimore. Photo courtesy of Wikimedia Commons.

Although Baltimore was never part of the Confederate States of America, many residents' sympathies were with the Rebel cause. The city was also known for street gangs and their criminal deeds. "Baltimore was the only city on Lincoln's itinerary where he had not been invited to speak," according to the article, "Lincoln's Epic Rail Journey to His First Inauguration," by Joe Gioia.

As the inauguration approached, Allan Pinkerton, who has been called America's first private detective, learned of a plot to kill Lincoln as he switched trains in Baltimore before he could become president. One of Pinkerton's agents, Kate Warne, the first female private detective, posed as a wealthy southern stockbroker and learned of the plot, which she relayed to Pinkerton. The plan involved one of the street gangs, led by a hotel barber from Corsica named Ferrandini, surrounding and stabbing Lincoln after diverting his guards.

Pinkerton didn't trust the police to protect the president-elect because he wasn't sure how prevalent anti-Union sentiment was in the police force.

Pinkerton came up with a plan to move Lincoln through the city earlier than the times on the published itinerary.

"Though the detective had been in contact with Lincoln's chief bodyguard, the president-elect was not told of the suspected plot until a security meeting with Pinkerton and others in Philadelphia," Gioia wrote.

Lincoln was ready to dismiss the plot as a rumor until an Army intelligence report arrived that confirmed much of what Pinkerton had said.

After Lincoln gave a speech in Harrisburg, Pa., he slipped away on a special three-car express to Philadelphia. Pinkerton met Lincoln and his bodyguard there. From there, they traveled to Baltimore with Lincoln incognito.

"Back at the station just minutes before the scheduled departure, the president-elect's party, now including detective Warne, who had reserved a private sleeper for her 'invalid brother' at the rear of the train, finally left for Baltimore," Gioia wrote.

The train arrived in Baltimore at 3 a.m. Lincoln's car was decoupled, horses pulled it through town on a tense 45-minute journey. It was then attached to a B&O Railroad train for the journey into Washington, D.C.

"This incident became one of the first major tests of Lincoln's presidency—even before it officially began," Gioia wrote.

The plot was possible only because there was no direct connection between the Western Maryland Railway and the Baltimore and Ohio Railroad in Baltimore.

Brass knuckles carried by one of Abraham Lincoln's bodyguards during his train ride through Baltimore. Photo courtesy of the Library of Congress.

Cutting Through the Problem

Although railroads replaced canals in the U. S. as a primary mode of transportation in the mid-1800s, that doesn't mean canals couldn't teach railroads a lesson or two in how to keep running. One of those lessons involves dealing with bitter winters and the ice they can bring that, left alone, will entirely stop traffic along a canal or a railroad.

The Chesapeake and Ohio Canal had special ice-breaking boats it used when cold winter temperatures started freezing the water in the canal. These specially-designed boats that were shorter than typical canal boats and heavily weighted with iron-reinforced bows. The canal mules pulled them along the canal as they would any boat, but ice-breaks were designed to slide up on top of the ice and break it the boat's weight. Some were fitted with removable plow blades that would help cut through the ice.

Likewise, when ice covered the tracks of the Western Maryland Railway or sealed tunnels, the railroad brought out its version of ice breakers.

The tunnels along the railroad, in particular, posed problems. The tunnels were wet in good weather. Water soaked through the ground, dripping into the tunnels, running down the tunnel sides, and collecting in pools. If a train passed through a tunnel, knocking icicles off the ceiling, it could damage tall cargo, such as automobiles stacked in multiple levels on a rail car. It was a liability against the Western Maryland Railway.

"During the winter months, this water froze in the tunnels, forcing track gangs to chip ice from the tracks and knock icicles off tunnel ceilings to prevent injury to train crews or damage to rolling stock," Dave Eckman wrote in The Blue Mountain Express.

Some of these icicles might be 18 inches thick, and although they didn't interfere with the engine, autorack cars had a higher clearance, and they damaged windshields or the auto bodies.

At 2,351 feet above sea level the Big Savage Tunnel between Frostburg, Md., and Meyersdale, Pa., was one of the worst places this happened. The Western Maryland Railway built the 3,294-foot-long tunnel in 1911 as part of the Connellsville Extion from Cumberland, Md. to Connellsville, Pa.

"Track gangs could not keep up with icicles forming there cold weather," Eckman wrote.

The Western Maryland Railway personnel brainstormed ideas and came up with the plan for an ice-breaker car in 1962. A boxcar built in 1937 was modified for a new purpose.

"Essentially, the shop forces torched the sides out of the car, leaving the frame and the ends intact," Eckman wrote. "Steel beams were then riveted together to provide support and bracing for a steel cutting bar extending across the width of the 'A' or leading end of car."

The reinforced angled steel cutting bar was 18 feet above the tracks and "shaped like a letter 'C' lying on its open face." The bracing angled back 45 degrees from the cutting bar.

The modified car weighed 49,500, which could be too light for some of the work it would be needed to do, so it was ballasted with 92,700 pounds of limestone slabs on the floor of the car. "The ballasting enabled the car to absorb the shock of impacts with large ice masses and brought its total weight to 142,200 pounds."

This first ice breaker was completed in May 1962 and

placed into service that winter. It was placed in front of the autorack cars on trains traveling between Cumberland and Connellsville. It removed the icicles before they could damage any cargo.

The first ice breaker was so successful, the railroad ordered a second one to be built. It was placed in service during the winter of 1963-1964. Both continued to be used until the Western Maryland Railroad trains started using Baltimore and Ohio Railroad parallel tracks in 1976.

What a Difference
a Letter Makes

Port Covington is best known for its use as a Western Maryland Railway terminal at the Chesapeake Bay. Cargo could be transferred from trains to waiting ships to be taken to anyplace with a seaport. Port Covington was built in 1904 and included coal, grain and merchandise piers, overhead cranes, rail yards, warehouses, a roundhouse, a turntable, and a machine shop. In the 1920s, rotary dumpers for coal and coke were installed, and a large grain elevator.

However, the massive port also helped defend the fledging United States defend itself against foreign invaders a century earlier.

Well, it wasn't Port Covington, but change one letter and you get Fort Covington, which was located on the same property at the port.

In the summer of 1813, the United States government built Fort Covington as a shore fortification to guard the ferry approach to Baltimore and aid neighboring Fort McHenry. The U.S. had entered a second war with the British the previous year and was struggling to hold on to what it had won during the Revolutionary War.

"Baltimore City officials, sensing Baltimore's vulnerability to a British attack, requested reinforcements from the War Department to fortify the city's defenses because Fort McHenry could not repulse the enemy alone," according to the Maryland Center for History and Culture website.

Fort Covington was a V shaped, 10-foot-tall brick enclosure designed to keep the British from outflanking Fort McHenry. In front of the enclosure was a 16-foot-tall ditch and parapet designed to hold 10 to 12 18-pound cannons mounted en barbette. There were also quarters for a company of soldiers and a powder magazine. It was small, even for a fort.

According to the Maryland in the War of 1812 blog, the fort was originally called Fort Patapsco, but after Brig. Gen. Leonard Covington, a Marylander, was killed at the Battle of Chrysler's Field in Upper Canada on November 11, 1813, the Maryland fort was renamed in his honor.

The first men to garrison there were Capt. Matthew S. Bunbury's U.S. Sea Fencibles. They were replaced during the Battle of Baltimore with Lt. Henry S. Newcomb's naval company.

As the Battle of Baltimore approached, the British were riding high on their successful campaign. In August 1814, the British had burned Washington, D.C., destroying the White House and U.S. Capitol in the process.

Then they moved towards Baltimore, hoping to destroy it and cut off trade through the city's port. On September 12, British and American troops fought at North Point and Hampstead Hill.

The next day, British warships began bombarding Fort McHenry and continued to do so for 25 hours.

"On the wind-swept stormy night of Sept, 13 Fort Covington, along with nearby Battery Babcock and Fort Look-Out, successfully repulsed a British flotilla advance having past (sic) to the west of Fort McHenry. The advance was checked and the British withdrew to the safety of the fleet in the outer harbor," according to the Maryland in the War of 1812 blog.

Fort McHenry withstood the bombardment, and the British were forced to retreat. The bombardment inspired Maryland lawyer Francis Scott Key, who was being held on a British ship. The sight of the American flag still flying over Fort McHenry after the bombardment inspired him to write a poem entitled "Defence of Fort M'Henry." This was later set to music and became our National Anthem, "The Star-Spangled Banner."

The Battle of Baltimore also proved to be a turning point in the war which ended the following year.

After the war, a minimal detachment was kept at Fort Covington until 1836, when all the material at the fort was sold at public auction.

As Baltimore expanded its borders, the fort and surrounding land became more integrated into the city.

The Western Maryland Railway had long wanted to connect its railroad network with the Baltimore harbor and the land around the former Fort Covington to be the perfect location. In 1883, the Western Maryland Tidewater Railroad Company which intended to build a tidewater line to bring goods from Walbrook Junction into the port, but the project stalled for nearly 20 years. The connecting line was completed in 1902, and Port Covington was completed in 1904. The construction of the terminal allowed the Western Maryland Railway to become a global operation.

Its nearness to the harbor made it an attractive spot for businesses that needed water access, such as shipyards and wharfs. Despite this, the surrounding land still remained relatively rural. Port Covington served as the southernmost border of the city until 1919.

However, the port slowly changed the area's landscape, and the city grew around the port's edges.

Port Covington operated into the 1970s, and the site was finally abandoned in 1988.

Does Anybody Know What Time It Is?

Ask a dozen Western Maryland Railway employees what time it was, and they would have looked at their pocket watches and given you a precise time. They also all might have been different, but they all would have been correct.

Taking about a trip from Baltimore on the Western Maryland Railway, Harold A. Williams wrote in The Western Maryland Railway Story, besides dealing with the normal issues of railway travel, such as making any connecting trains, "the individual time system used by the railroads which must have bewildered and bedeviled all but the most experienced traveler."

In the early days of rail travel, railroads used about 100 different times. "When it was 10 a.m. Western Maryland time, it might be 10:05 or 9:55 on other roads connecting with it," Williams wrote.

This would be confusing for anyone, especially an infrequent rail traveler.

Williams used the example of an 1875 timetable that ran a notice above the timetable that read, "Leaving Baltimore, Baltimore time is used. Philadelphia time (five minutes faster than Baltimore time) is used at other stations."

This is because cities and towns ran on local time based on their geographic location. It was imprecise, but in the mid-1800s, towns were still somewhat isolated and travel tended to be slow, so knowing the time where you were going wasn't that important if it would take you a day to get there.

Railroads changed that. They moved more quickly, and so knowing the time where you were going became more important.

A Western Maryland train waiting at a station. Photo courtesy of Wikimedia Commons.

Beyond the passenger inconvenience, time was just as important for the people running the trains. On a single track, if the engineer or someone else got the time wrong, he might send two trains hurtling at each other. A good example of this is the Blue Mountain Express wreck near Sabillasville, Md., in 1915. The Blue Mountain Express was running 20 minutes late when it reached Thurmont on June 25. The engineer was doing his best to make up lost time. The train dispatcher lost an order that countermanded the train's right of way since it was running late. The Baltimore Unlimited, which now had the right of way on a twenty-mile-line run of single track, collided with the Blue Mountain Express on a bridge, killing six people and severely injuring twelve.

To avoid these accidents, communication was key, but to avoid creating the situation where an accident could happen, timing was everything.

The timetables and watches conductors always seemed to consult were visible aspects of this. Workers compared the time on their pocket watches to the time on a master clock often. They also compared the time on their watches to those on other watches often. The frequent checks helped account for a watch that might be running fast or slow.

"By the mid-1800s, railroads operated far-flung systems with split-second timing while the rest of the country considered the measurement of time's passage a purely local affair. Each community set its own time, often based on when the sun crossed the meridian when viewed from a local landmark," according to an article on Trains.com.

This had problems because time could vary depending on your location.

"Passengers in Buffalo, N.Y., were confronted by three station clocks. One was set to New York City time, the standard used by the New York Central RR. The second showed Columbus time for the convenience of Lake Shore & Michigan Southern passengers. And the third clock indicated local Buffalo time," according to Trains.com.

Time systems could also be problematic because with different rail lines using different systems, a city served by multiple railroads would need clocks set to their time systems and clearly marked.

In November 1840, the Great Western Railway in England synchronized the local times to a single standard time. It greatly reduced the confusion in dealing with local times and near misses. Over the next seven years, the other railroads in

England adopted the system.

As the U.S. railroads recognized the advantages of the uniform time system, they became more organized. Charles Dowd proposed four time zones - Eastern, Central, Mountain and Pacific–across the U.S. that all railroads could use.

William F. Allen, secretary of the American Railroad Association, announced that U.S. railroads would adopt this system on November 18, 1883. Once the railroads across the country started using the system, it didn't take long for local communities to realize that it was a simpler system that made sense, and they adopted it as well.

Congress officially adopted standard time for the country in 1918.

Two Uses For the Price of One

The Western Maryland Railway once had a train station in a grain elevator.

Grain elevators were buildings used to store grain. The elevator part was a method used to raise the grain up to top of a silo. They often used a Dart elevator, invented by Joseph Dart and Robert Dunbar in 1842. It was originally designed to scoop grain out of ship holds and carry it the top of a marine tower. The early grain elevators carried the grain in wooden boxes, which made them fire hazards.

Keymar, Md., began as a small settlement called Bruceville, which was part of Frederick County at the time. Normand Bruce, who emigrated from Scotland in 1762, laid out a town on Big Pipe Creek that he named after himself in 1763.

That year, the State of Maryland granted 5,301 acres from Keysville, Md., to north of Bruceville, a region called "Bedford," to Bruce and Edward Diggs. At the same time, John Ross Key already owned land south of Big Pipe Creek. His property, "Terra Rubra," was the birthplace of Francis Scott Key in 1779.

Bruce's goal was to build a mill along the creek, which led to Key and Bruce developing a working relationship and their families intermixing.

Francis Scott Key became famous for writing the poem, "The Defence of Fort M'Henry," following the War of 1812. It was eventually set to music, renamed "The Star-Spangled Banner," and became the National Anthem in 1931. Bruceville was renamed Keymar, in honor of Key and his role in the War of 1812 in 1822 (Some sources say this change did not happen officially happen until 1917). However, Keymar was still not much more than a few homes, a mill, a coach shop, blacksmith, school, store and a resident physician. It was also located on the dirt road that was main road between Hanover, Pa., and Frederick, Md.

Even when the Western Maryland Railroad reached the town in 1868, Keymar had only a few houses, a sawmill, a bonemill, and a small brick grain warehouse that also served as the post office. The population was fewer than 60 people. According to the Blue Mountain Express, "the town was not very important to anyone except its residents."

Because the grain elevator was most important building in the village, it became the train station.

Frederick, feeling that the railroad might bypass them, decided to build its own connecting railroad from the city. "As a result, the Frederick and Pennsylvania Line Railroad Company was formed. Evidently, the idea to build to the Littlestown RR in Littlestown, Pa., was an afterthought," according to the Blue Mountain Express.

The line traveled from Frederick to the Maryland towns of Fountain Rock, Walkersville, Woodsboro, LeGore, Renner's (New Midway), Ladiesburg, Keymar, and Taneytown, before it stopped in Littlestown. It reached Keymar in 1871, connecting with the Western Maryland Railroad.

At that time, it is believed the grain elevator stopped functioning in that capacity and strictly became a building serving as two train depots.

Becoming Part of "The Syndicate"

The Western Maryland Railroad entered its modern age on May 7, 1902. That was the day that the Baltimore City government, under the leadership of Mayor Thomas G. Hayes voted to sell its interests in the railroad to the Fuller Syndicate.

That changed unleashed a period of unprecedented growth for the railroad.

"By 1912, the Western Maryland had doubled its mileage and business and had become a busy trunk line, linking the Great Lakes, the Midwest and the coal fields of Western Maryland with the eastern seaboard," Harold A. Williams wrote in *The Western Maryland Railway Story*.

The growth didn't come because Baltimore had been holding the railroad back. In its early decades, the Western Maryland Railroad had often depended on its support from Baltimore City to make it through tough financial times. For its help, the city got a favorable rate compared to other port cities like Philadelphia and Baltimore. The railroad also gave the city a preference as it tried to develop its port. However, the burden of financing the railroad weighed heavily on the city finances, and the city had considered divesting itself of the railroad as early as 1877.

However, with Baltimore divesting itself, other investors saw a chance to get into the railroad business.

Bids from interested buyers were solicited and four groups submitted. Among them was the Fuller Syndicate, a group of American financiers who invested in railroads. Edward Laton Fuller, President of the International Salt Company, organized the group.

George W. Gould led the group. He had inherited several railroads from his father Jay Gould. Other members of the syndicate included Myron T. Herrick, former Governor of Ohio and U.S. Ambassador to France; Winslow S. Pierce, General Counsel of the Gould organization; Joseph Ramsey, Jr., president of the Wabash Railroad; and Alvin W. Krech, vice president of the Wheeling and Lake Erie Railroad.

The Fuller Syndicate not only faced stiff competition from other railroads, but Gould had an urge to form a transcontinental railroad. The Western Maryland Railroad would form the eastern link in that chain of railroads.

The four bidders for Baltimore's shares were: Hambleton & Company for $10 million ($6 million in cash, $4 million in stock), the Reading Railway Company for $7,004,099 in cash (later increased to $10,001,000), William W. Varney for $11 million ($3 million in cash in 90 days, $2 million in cash two years later, and $6 million in 5 percent income bonds), and the Fuller Syndicate for $8,509,820 (later increased to $8,751,370.45).

The Fuller Syndicate also guaranteed full repayment of the Western Maryland indebtedness to the city, a rail line from Big Pool to Cumberland to connect the railroad with the West Virginia Central, and a tidewater terminal. Although the Fuller Syndicate did not offer the highest bid, these promises offered other advantages that the Baltimore City Council and Mayor Hayes found attractive. Abstracts from the city council reports noted:

"Gentlemen named as the bidders are backed by perhaps the most powerful financial connections in the United States. These connections control the Wabash Railroad, the Wheeling and Lake Erie Road, and the West Virginia Central. Each of these roads forms a link in a chain of gigantic traffic combinations extending from the Pacific Coast to the Atlantic. They desire the Western Maryland to make the chain complete. Their roads drain fertile valleys and rich coal and lumber fields, which, while earning for themselves a handsome profit, will yield to Baltimore a splendid opportunity to regain her lost commercial prestige. Here, in our opinion, as well as in the opinion of the Chamber of Commerce, is a splendid opportunity to build anew the grain trade, which a short time ago, was the envy of sister cities and the glory of our merchants. Therefore it is our opinion that if we desire the maintenance and development of Baltimore's commercial and industrial prestige, ever consideration points to the acceptance of the Fuller bid."

The Fuller Syndicate gained full control of the Western Maryland Railroad in 1906, and the syndicate began an era of aggressive expansion.

At its peak, the Fuller Syndicate reached from San Francisco to Pittsburgh. It included:

- Western Pacific Railway
- Rio Grande Western Railway
- Denver and Rio Grande Railroad
- Missouri Pacific Railroad
- Wabash Railroad
- Wheeling and Lake Erie Railroad
- Wabash Pittsburgh Terminal Railway
- Western Maryland Railroad

However, this extensive system of railroads had a 150-mile gap between Pittsburgh and Connellsville, Pennsylvania, that kept it from being a transcontinental railroad. The State Line and Southern Railroad was chartered in 1910 to bridge the gap, and later the Pittsburgh and West Virginia Railroad was also intended to bridge the gap.

The plan fell apart after the Knickerbocker Crisis in 1907 when the New York Stock Exchange lost half its value of three weeks in October. The country was already in a recession and this drop in value caused many banks and businesses to go into bankruptcy. The effect on the financiers as well as the Western Maryland Railroad caused it to go into receivership on March 5, 1908, until December 31, 1909.

However, the Fuller Syndicate continued to work and improve the railroad once it came out of receivership.

Odds & Ends

Rain vs. Rail

On June 22, 1972, Hurricane Agnes hit the East Coast, causing $2.1 billion in damage and taking 128 lives. While Pennsylvania was the hardest hit state, nearby Maryland suffered nearly as much. It was the costliest hurricane in U.S. history at that time and so devastating that the name Agnes for hurricanes was retired in 1973.

Agnes dumped more than 10 inches of rain on Maryland and Pennsylvania. Rivers flooded, and the storm surge was so bad that some rivers temporarily had their flows reversed.

It was the first named storm of the 1972 Atlantic hurricane season. It formed as a tropical depression on June 14 over the Yucatan Peninsula. It moved over the Caribbean Sea and strengthened into Tropical Storm Agnes. As it moved northward over the water, it strengthened into a hurricane.

It made landfall near Panama City, Florida, on June 19. It quickly weakened as it moved across Florida into Georgia and South Carolina. However, it strengthened again over eastern North Carolina. It moved over the Atlantic maintaining its strength. It made landfall again on at New York City on June 22.

Amid all the wind and rain, the Western Maryland Railway (as well as all railroads in the path of the hurricane) also suffered damage. As Agnes moved back out to the ocean, it left behind a railroad that could not operate beyond Hagerstown.

"Tropical Storm Agnes clobbered the Western Maryland leaving an eight-mile gap in the railroad's main stem and punctuating the end of the modern-day independent as we knew it," according to the Blue Mountain Express. In one area, the water rose nine feet in fifteen minutes.

Some of the damage to the Western Maryland Railway that Hurricane Agnes left behind. Photo courtesy of the Western Maryland Railway Historical Society.

Here is a list of the some of the significant damage along the Western Maryland Railway:

• Bridges and the roadbed were washed out along Pipe Creek.

• Much of the track along the Patapsco River was washed out.

• A concrete bridge at Owings Mills, Md., and more than 100 feet of roadbed approaching the bridge were destroyed.

• Gwynn Falls surge and flooding took out miles of track leading to Port Covington at the Baltimore waterfront.

• At Cedarhurst, Md., loaded box cars were moved as if they were branches. One box car was found over three miles away from where it had been on the tracks.

• More than three feet of water covered the tracks at Chambersburg, Pa.

Despite all this damage, it could have been worse for the Western Maryland Railway. No lives were lost. No trains were left marooned, and only a few of the fixed facilities were flooded.

Damaged track and torn open box cars caused by Hurricane Agnes. Photo courtesy of the Western Maryland Railway Historical Society.

"Western Maryland employees responded like a well-trained military unit. There was little dramatic heroism but a great deal of hard work and long hours," according to the Blue Mountain Express.

Within two days, much of the damage had been cleaned up or repaired. The Lurgan line was the first section to reopen. Then the area around Porters Sideling, Pa., opened to service to York, Pa. On June 28, Porters Sideling to Emory Grove, Md. opened and Highfield, Md., to Union Bridge, Md.

The Blue Mountain Express reported that at one area flooding had apparently carried four homes off their foundations into the railroad right of way. Workers used cranes to lift the homes onto rollers and blocks to carefully move them out of the way.

More of the damage to the Western Maryland Railway that Hurricane Agnes left behind. Photo courtesy of the Western Maryland Railway Historical Society.

A new steel bridge was constructed at Owings Mills,

Md., to replace the concrete one.

Once things were operational again, things could move at a more measured pace. Permanent structures and roadbed replaced any temporary fixes that had been used in the rush to restore service. Slowly things once again moved back to normalcy.

Cumberland's Bone Cave

In *Back to the Future, Part III*, Doc Brown invents a time machine out of a locomotive. Perhaps, the idea came from the Western Maryland Railway, which in the beginning of the 20th century was in a respect, a time machine that could take someone 200,000 years into the past.

In 1912, the Western Maryland Railway was in the midst of a large expansion. It had finally reached Cumberland, Md., in 1906, and soon thereafter, construction began on the Connellsville Extension from Cumberland to Connellsville, Pa. To make that connection, the track needed to go through the Allegheny Mountains.

As the workers excavated a cut along the side of Will's Mountain, they blasted through the cut, widening it to allow trains to pass. At one point near Corriganville, Md., a steam shovel uncovered a small cave on the north end of a limestone ridge.

"It was not the size or beauty of the cave that attracted attention, because the underground room was neither impressive in magnitude nor appearance," J. William Hunt wrote in The (Cumberland) Sunday Times. What caused workmen to comment was the extensive collection of bones and animal skeletons uncovered."

The cave descended at a 45-degree angle and it is believed an extinct stream may have deposited silt and clay containing the remains into the cave through its original entrance, a sinkhole on the top of the ridge.

A local naturalist named Raymond Armbruster heard

about the discovery. He visited the site and examined the cave and the debris that had been removed. Besides the abundance of bones, he found other fossils in the rocks. Unfortunately, because the workers were blasting through the cut with dynamite, some of the fossils were shattered.

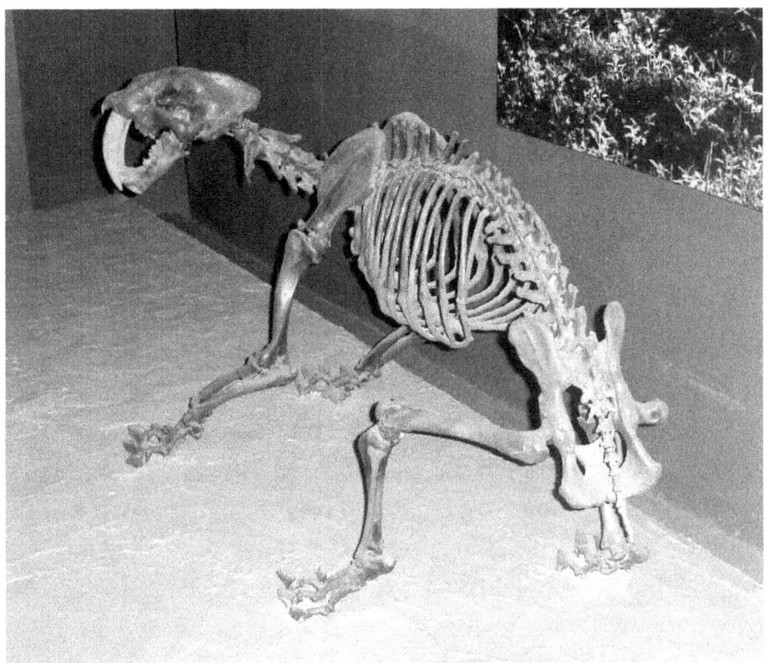

The skeleton of a saber-tooth tiger found in Cumberland's Bone Cave. Photo courtesy of Wikimedia Commons.

Armbruster sent some of the fossils and bones to the Smithsonian Institution with a letter explaining the cave find.

"The arrival of those fossils from Cumberland caused almost as much excitement in the staid scientific circles of the Smithsonian as the atomic bomb caused in World War II," Hunt wrote.

This was only the third known cave in North America to

contain such a wealth of Pleistocene remains. The other two caves are the Conrad Fissure in Alabama and the Port Kennedy Cave in Pennsylvania. The Cumberland Bone Cave has the greater number of mammalian species found, but the other caves have a greater number of total species found.

James W. Gidley was sent to examine the cave. Gidley spent four years excavating the cave and found the bones from 41 different genera of mammals, of which 20 percent were extinct. Some of them are as old as 200,000 years. Other fossils were from birds and invertebrates. Gidley even found enough bones to reconstruct some of the animals. He called it one of the most important natural discoveries of the 20th century.

"Skeletons from what is known as the 'Cumberland' Cave Bear and an extinct Saber-toothed cat are on permanent exhibit at the National Museum of Natural History. Other fauna identified here include mastodons, coyotes, pumas and even a crocodile," according to the Historical Marker Database.

Included among the remains found in the cave were wolverine, coyote, crocodile, porcupine, muskrat, elk, mink, tapir, black bear, horse, badger, jumping mice, bats, peccaries, puma, gopher, and mastodon.

Once the original exploration of the cave was completed, the Western Maryland Railway sealed the cave for safety reasons.

Not much of the cave still exists, but the Maryland Department of Natural Resources continues to excavate it, looking for new discoveries.

The Snallygaster at the Railroad

Scotland has Nessie, and the American Northwest has Bigfoot. They are legendary monsters. The Middletown Valley has its own monster called the snallygaster.

Snallygasters have been reported in Maryland for centuries. Some people believe the name has German origins. "Schnelle geist" means "fast ghost."

Initially, snallygasters were reptilian birds that preyed on poultry and children.

Frederick County's snallygaster is decidedly nastier.

On February 12, 1909, folks around Middletown, Md., opened their newspapers to read that a large winged creature had swooped down and carried off a man walking along the road. The beast then sucked out most of the man's blood and tossed the empty carcass aside.

"And either the folks in Western Maryland were unusually impressionable or there really was something terrible on the loose, because within hours of the first appearance in the Register, people in Frederick and Washington Counties and even nearby Shepherdstown, West Virginia, began reporting encounters with the flying monster," Susan Fair wrote in *Legends and Lore of Western Maryland*. A man from Casstown, Ohio, wrote in the same issue and called the creature a snallygaster.

Descriptions vary, but once you saw it, you would definitely remember it. Dragonlike, long wings, long pointed tail, sometimes with a horn, one eye in the middle of its forehead, octopus-like tentacles that trailed behind like streamers, retractable claws. Some reports noted that the claws were razor sharp. One woman said the snallygaster had hoofs. A man named George Jacobs said he shot at the snallygaster while hunting. Fair wrote, "…the monster apparently didn't care for being shot at. As a matter of fact, it was so annoyed that it pursued Jacobs across a field, all the while lunging angrily— or perhaps hungrily—at the terrified man's neck."

The *Hagerstown Mail* said that the Smithsonian Institution wanted to examine the creature. The *Middletown Valley Register* reported that the military was sending in soldiers armed with Gatling guns.

A painting of the snallygaster making off with a cow. Photo courtesy of Wikimedia Commons.

President Theodore Roosevelt was said to be considering a big-game hunt in Africa to stalk an even greater prize in the snallygaster.

People around Middletown were terrified. Harry Wachtel

of Myersville, Md., shot and wounded what he thought was the snallygaster.

It turned out to be a large owl.

"Some say it is a Canadian owl, some say it is just a 'booby owl,' but all agree that with its weird gray wings spread in the cold dead of night it would be taken for a 'snallygaster,' 'jabberwock,' 'wampdoodle' or another terrifying species," the *Frederick Post* reported.

The snallygaster appeared throughout the Middletown Valley, on South Mountain, on Catoctin Mountain, and even as far west as Cumberland, Md., where the snallygaster spoke for the first time.

It reportedly attacked a man there and said, "My, I'm dry! I haven't had a good drink since I was killed in the Battle of Chickamauga." With that report, people started wondering if the creature was a reincarnated Civil War soldier.

In Sharpsburg, Md., it was reported that the nest of eggs from the creature was found.

The Western Maryland Railway also played a small role in the story through its connection with the Emmitsburg Railroad. In the February 26, 1909, edition of The (Emmitsburg) Weekly Chronicle, the snallgaster supposedly tried to grab Ed Brown, a worker on the Emmitsburg Railroad. The beast caught him, but lucky for Brown, his suspender snapped, and he got away. A mob pursued the snallygaster, which then displayed a new skill—shooting fire from its nostrils.

Bill Snyder, a witness to the event described the snallygaster this way: "It looked like a giraffe on rollerskates. Its beak was serrated with great tusks and between them lay the partially consumed flesh of a colored man nearly putrid. Its snout resemble a silo and from the corners of its mouth leaked a fluid like melted limestone."

Over the years, it has become apparent that this story was probably the work of a group of Emmitsburg residents who met regularly at the Hotel Slagle and came up with unusual stories that the newspaper published. The group consisted of Jacob Turner, Jerry Overholser, Daniel Shorb, and Bill Snyder, along with Sterling Galt, editor of the *Emmitsburg Chronicle*. Their stories are usually identifiable by their fantastical details.

In this story, when the original story is found, it includes Ed Brown counting each piece of a pile of coal in the railroad coal bunkers and discovering that it was 16 pieces short. He thought this might be due to coal shrinkage at the rate of "D, minyum charge 2-8 per ounce."

Another detail mentioned was that Snyder said when the snallygaster arrived it sounded like "Flat Run at high tide where the waters rush over the rocks at Whitmore's warf, only more so." Flat Run is non-tidal and doesn't have a wharf.

If that wasn't enough, two of the "witnesses" were Dan Shorb and Bill Snyder. This is another sign of one of the group's stories: They often placed themselves in the story.

While most of the group's stories were wildly original, this one was apparently building on another fiction writer's work.

Thomas Harbaugh was the Ohio man who first referenced the snallygaster. He was a native of Middletown, though. He was also the author of 650 "nickel novels." I guess they were only half as good as dime novels. He was also good friends with the *Register* editor, George Rhoderick.

"All it took was one little story, and local residents—not to mention reporters and editors of competing newspapers—were ready to release their inner monsters, collaborating on a creation that gleefully took on a life of its own," Fair suggested.

A drawing of the snallygaster based on witness descriptions. Courtesy of Wikimedia Commons.

A Rose By Any Other Name

McDaniel College in Westminster, Md., owes its existence to the Western Maryland Railroad, but it didn't want to be known for its connection to the railroad or even the western end of the state.

When the college opened in 1867, it was Western Maryland College, named after the Western Maryland Railroad. This is because John Smith, the first chairman of the college board, was also a former president of the railroad. Smith served less than a year as the president of the Western Maryland Railroad from November 6, 1862, to July 6, 1863. Although the college is named after the railroad, the railroad did not contribute funds to establish it.

For much of its history, Western Maryland College had a voluntary fraternal affiliation with the Methodist Protestant (later United Methodist) Church from 1868 until 1974. This ended due to a court case that challenged religiously affiliated schools in Maryland eligibility to receive state funding because of their religious ties. Although Western Maryland College cut its religious ties, the schools that continued their affiliations won the case.

The first class to enter the college in September 1867 was made up of 37 students. It was among one of the first co-educational colleges in the country.

In early 2002, it was announced that school officials had voted in April, after input from students, faculty, and alumni, to rename Western Maryland College as McDaniel College after Williams Roberts McDaniel. He had attended the college in the late 1870s and gone on to serve as a professor, treasurer, acting president, and trustee for the school. His affiliation with the school spanned 65 years.

"We name this college for a person whose life was changed here on the Hill, a person who, in turn, changed lives," College President Joan Develin Coley said. "He was one of us."

A scan of an old postcard showing Western Maryland College.

It was said that a name change had been discussed for decades because the name Western Maryland College created confusion. People apparently thought the college was located in western, rather than central, Maryland.

"The college first was named for a railroad, which no longer exists," Coley said.

However, the name change was not without controversy. An Associated Press report read, "The name change sparked protests from some students and alumni who said a new moniker would 'erase' the history of the school."

The name change became official on July 1, 2002.

Pen Mar was a Popular Spot for Moonshiners

When the federal government banned the sale, production, and transportation of alcohol in the United States in 1919, citizens had to choose between becoming teetotalers or criminals. Many law-abiding citizens chose the latter.

Since a person could get in trouble buying a drink, people who did it didn't talk about it. That didn't mean that it wasn't happening. Underground bars, or speakeasies, weren't advertised. People knew about them by word of mouth. You got in by knowing someone or knowing a password. Manufacturing moved to stills hidden in the woods or basements.

Moonshining (the illegal manufacture or distribution of alcohol) has been around since the Whiskey Rebellion in the 1790s. The Western Pennsylvanians who refused to pay the federal taxes on homemade liquor were the country's first moonshiners.

However, it wasn't until the Prohibition era that moonshining took off because the demand for alcohol increased. With the profits rising—a quart of moonshine could fetch $16 ($225 in today's dollars) in Hagerstown, Md.—, more and more people were willing to risk being arrested and became moonshiners, rumrunners, bootleggers.

Moonshining in Pen Mar

Pen Mar Park, with its ideal location as a resort on the border between Maryland and Pennsylvania, became a favorite spot for bootleggers to hide their stills. Also, being at Pen Mar put them close to people who wanted to relax and enjoy themselves with a drink. In 1921, an informant told police that there were thirteen stills that he knew of near Pen Mar. The bootleggers were making a lot of money selling their product, though they didn't stay long in one place.

Blue Mountain House at Pen Mar was a popular tourist destination during Prohibition, which meant local bootleggers had a large customer base. Photo courtesy of the Library of Congress.

The *Gettysburg Compiler* reported that one informant about the bootlegging at Pen Mar saw "a bootlegger with a suitcase, placed the latter on a rock near the old Blue Mountain House path and did a land office business by handing the liquor out by the pint and half pint to people who appeared from among the bushes."

After a few minutes, he closed up shop, disappeared into

the woods only to reappear in another location about half an hour later.

In 1925 revenuers tried to get Daniel Toms' 30-gallon still in Cascade. He held them off for a short time with a shotgun, but they eventually surrounded him and caught him and his henchmen.

Smithsburg Moonshining War

Revenuers also spent plenty of time in Smithsburg combing the hills for moonshiners. They tried to pass themselves off as tourist hikers.

Smithsburg also made national headlines as having an "old-time mountain feud" between John Cline and Henry Russman involving night raiding, indiscriminate shooting, and fights. They were accused of wrecking a church, dynamiting a sawmill, killing one person, and wounding others. A 1923 article estimated that there were 500 stills between Hagerstown and the Pennsylvania line. The interest in this fighting may have been due in part to the recent coal mine riots that had grown so violent across the country.

"They are unmolested. It would be as much as an officer's life would be worth to try and interfere. The natives are silent. They know a bullet in the dark would follow any giving of information," the *Hagerstown Mail* reported.

Thurmont Moonshining

Former Catoctin Mountain Park Ranger Debra Mills explained that Catoctin Mountain was much more barren during the Prohibition era and the people who lived on it were impoverished.

"Prohibition was probably a good thing economically for people in this area," Mills said.

Having stills operating nearby gave farmers a place to

sell their crops. Although corn was the most popular grain for moonshine, Elmer Black of Thurmont said in a 2015 interview that he only ever knew of rye being raised to sell to the local moonshiners in the area.

The remnants of a still on Catoctin Mountain. Photo courtesy of the Catoctin Mountain Park photo archives.

The finished product was often shipped out of the area on the railroad in barrels labeled cornmeal, according to Mills.

It could leave other ways as well. Black recalled that his grandfather would often run moonshine right under the nose of the county sheriff and his deputies. He would get the family together to take a ride in their Studebaker and off they would go. There was an ulterior motive for the drive, though. He had hidden moonshine underneath the seats.

"My grandfather would wave 'hi' as they went by the sheriff," Black said.

Two of Black's uncles were some of the most-successful bootleggers around the Thurmont, Md., area. Even his father was known to drive moonshine out of the region to sell. One time he took Black and his sibling along for the ride. The kids fell asleep.

"The three of us woke up and asked who lives here," Black said. "Some senator they told us. They were rolling the barrels up to the house."

They were hidden on the mountain near streams that could supply them with the water needed for the moonshine recipes. According to Black, if you follow the streams on Catoctin Mountain upriver, you can still see the remnants of destroyed stills.

Martin shared some of his family stories during a presentation at the Thurmont Regional Library in 2016 about moonshining.

One grandfather kept a quarter keg of moonshine in his attic, and when friends would come by with Mason jars, Martin's grandfather would tell his son to go up and get some 'shine for the friends.

At some point, Martin's grandfather moved the keg from the attic to the basement and buried it in the coal pile.

Once, revenue agents came by wanting to search the house while Martin's father was alone. The boy didn't know what to do because he couldn't get on the phone to call his parents, so he let the revenue agents in to search the house.

They started in the attic which worried Martin's father, but the men found nothing. Martin's father thought he was safe and that the moonshine was no longer in the house. The revenue agents continued their search, ending up in the basement.

One agent saw the coal pile and wondered if moonshine might be buried in it. Martin's father, not knowing that was the case, held up the coal shovel and told the agents, "Go ahead and dig, but you've got to put it all back, or my dad will be mad."

Luckily, the agents were lazy and chose not to dig. Martin's grandfather moved the moonshine out of the house after that.

The revenue agents did eventually catch up with Martin's grandfather. According to Martin, they came in the front door of the house chasing Martin's grandfather while the man went out the back door. The federal agents chased after him.

Martin's father, a young boy at the time, chased after the men. "Dad, he caught up with one revenuer and bit him on the leg and my grandfather got away," Martin said.

End of an era

Due to its unpopularity, Prohibition soon ended after the election of Franklin D. Roosevelt in 1932. Everyone went out and drank to his health.

One President Committed Suicide

On Thursday evening, April 4, 1860, William Roberts ate a delicious dinner with his wife, Eleanor. During the meal, he told his wife he needed to visit his brother that evening. He kissed his wife goodbye and left the house to get his carriage.

That was the last Eleanor saw of her husband alive.

At some point, someone walked into the carriage house later and found Roberts hanging by the neck from rafters. He was dead, having committed suicide.

Roberts was the third president of the Western Maryland Railroad and, as the newspaper announcements of his death noted, "a gentleman of irreproachable moral character and steady habits."

No reason was ever given for why Roberts chose to end his life at 61 years old. He had no financial problems and his marriage was solid.

He was a man who valued education and learning. Edward M. Killough wrote in History of the Western Maryland Railway, that Roberts "was one of the first in Frederick County to have a library, and all of the people for many miles around would come to borrow his books."

He had served as president of the railroad since June 23, 1858. During his time in office, he signed the contract to begin construction of the railroad from Relay House to Union

Bridge.

With Roberts' death, the board of directors assumed control of the railroad as they sought out a replacement. They would eventually appoint a wealthy Carroll County banker named Augustus Shriver as the new president of June 12. 1860. He would be the first of four presidents to lead the Western Maryland Railroad through the Civil War.

Although Roberts called himself a life-long Carroll Countians, he was actually born in New Windsor in Frederick County, in 1799. "His ancestors were owners of original grants of land in and around Uniontown, then in Frederick County," according to FindaGrave.com.

However, Carroll County was formed from parts of Frederick and Baltimore counties in 1837, and New Windsor became part of Carroll County. Roberts had been one of the many residents who supported the creation of a new county and worked towards it.

"In the early part of 1833 a bill was introduced in the House of Delegates by William Cost Johnson, for the formation of Carroll County, and it passed both branches of the General Assembly. It was necessary, however, to have a majority of votes in the 1833 election in each segment of Baltimore and Frederick Counties (the two counties affected), and as election day approached, meetings were held for public discussion, and at a meeting held in Westminster a committee was appointed of persons living outside the town. William Roberts was a member of this committee," Killough wrote.

As an adult Roberts ran a successful store in Uniontown. He was then elected to the Maryland Senate, where he served six years as a Whig.

When he died he left behind not only his widow, but also three children–two daughters and a son. He is buried in the Uniontown Methodist Cemetery.

William Roberts' grave marker. Photo courtesy of Findagrave.com.

The Johnstown Flood Stopped the Railroad in its Tracks

On Memorial Day 1889, the South Fork Dam on the Little Conemaugh River in Cambria County, Pa., burst. Twenty million tons of water surged into the river to Johnstown, Pa., scraping much of the ground clean of trees, buildings, people and animals. The powerful wall of water killed over 2,000 people, making the Johnstown Flood one of the greatest disasters in American history. No one knew it at the time because the flooding knocked out telegraph lines at Johnstown.

That flood destroyed railroads throughout the area, including the Western Maryland Railroad. Luckily, it did not suffer as much damage as the Pennsylvania Railroad, which had a greater presence in Cambria County. The Western Maryland Railroad did not run to Johnstown, but the damage from that flood and the storm system that created it was felt throughout the region.

The Western Maryland Railroad's lines in the Cumberland–Connellsville region, which ran along the Youghiogheny River and connected toward Pittsburgh, sustained flood damage. The surging water washed out bridges, culverts, and sections of track along the route. Because the Western Maryland Railroad was building its Connellsville Extension during the 1880s, parts of that newly constructed infrastructure had to be rebuilt.

The Shepherdstown Register reported, "The Western Maryland Railroad was knocked completely out of time. A number of its bridges down in Carroll county were washed away, and great gaps in its embankments made. In the neighborhood of Mechanicstown there was great destruction also, and trains could not pass that point until Tuesday. Connection was made with Hagerstown by Gettysburg via its several branch lines."

Damage on Main Street left behind from the Johnstown Flood. Photo courtesy of Wikimedia Commons.

"The Western Maryland Railroad Company and their connecting lines, the Baltimore and Harrisburg, and the Cumberland Valley roads, lost heavily. On the mountain grades of the Blue Ridge there are tremendous washouts, and in some sections the tracks are torn up and the road-bed destroyed. Several bridges were washed away." Willis Fletcher Johnson wrote in History of the Johnstown Flood.

Service on the Western Maryland Railroad and its connections was suspended for days to weeks, depending on the location. Traffic between Cumberland and Connellsville was interrupted due to track washouts, bridge failures, and debris covering the right-of-way. Freight bound for Pittsburgh and the coal fields was delayed or rerouted.

The Western Maryland depended heavily on coal and freight interchange traffic with western lines. With the Pennsylvania Railroad and Baltimore & Ohio Railroad lines also badly damaged, regional freight movement was paralyzed. The Western Maryland Railroad lost revenue from halted coal shipments and the inability to move freight through to Pittsburgh markets.

Wrecked Pullman cars and engines from the Johnstown Flood. Courtesy of Wikimedia Commons.

Like other railroads, the Western Maryland Railroad had to spend heavily on repairs. Emergency work crews rebuilt bridges and track beds. This increased the company's expenses in the years following the disaster.

While the catastrophe at Johnstown grabbed headlines, the Western Maryland Railroad's own network in Maryland suffered days-to-weeks of disruption from washouts, lost bridges, and torn-up track—especially on its mountainous Blue Ridge stretches and along the Potomac—before service could be restored.

Edward M. Killough also noted in History of the Western Maryland Railway that because of the flood "traffic was suspended entirely over the West Virginia Central for two days, and over the Piedmont and Cumberland road for ten days."

A tree lodged in a wrecked home in the aftermath of the Johnstown Flood. Photo courtesy of Wikimedia Commons.

Too Many Mechanics

Although requests from the Western Maryland Railroad wasn't the only reason for Mechanicstown, Md., to change its name, it was a large reason for the name change.

The typical date for the founding of Mechanicstown is 1751, so it was already 120 years old when the Western Maryland Railroad reached the town on January 9, 1871. The railroad's arrival brought a new energy to the town, new visitors, and new businesses.

"Along with the old tanneries and mills, newer industries such as cigar-making, pottery, coffin works and lumber businesses shipped their goods from freight depot. The produce of its bountiful farms and orchards fed the cities. In return, some of the city dwellers escaped the heat and smells of summer to enjoy the clean air and mountain scenery of our town. The numerous daily trains brought sportsmen and hikers, but also summer boarders whose families returned year after year," Anne Cissel wrote in an article in *A Thurmont Scrapbook*.

As the town continued growing, businessmen in town began feeling "the old name was antiquated and smacked of a by-gone image," Cissell wrote. They wanted something that would reflect the area's scenic beauty and attract residents and businesses."

As a leading business in the town, the officers of the Western Maryland Railroad had their own reasons for wanting the town to change its name. They felt the names was too similar to other nearby towns like Mechanicsburg and Mechanicsville in Pennsylvania that had caused shipping and passenger mix-ups.

Not everyone agreed with this view. "What is wrong with the present name?" one citizen wrote in The Catoctin Clarion. "Has the town ceased to be a town of Mechanics? Will a better sounding name induce capital to invest among us? Is there a name that can be chosen that will awaken and arouse enthusiasm among the native born of the place as the old name, Mechanicstown, will?"

He pointed out that the Western Maryland Railroad officers hadn't complained about the name when the railroad arrived in Mechanicstown, nor had the people who had settled in the town over the previous 142 years.

The Western Maryland Railway Station in Thurmont, MD. Photo courtesy of Thurmontimages.com.

With this movement to rename the town, the Catoctin Clarion ran a contest seeking new names for Mechanicstown. The winner was Blue Mountain City, but the United States Postal Department nixed this idea because there was already a Blue Mountain Post Office. The name could have created the same problem for the postal department that the Western Maryland Railroad was trying to avoid. It might also have been confused with the nearby Blue Ridge Summit in Pennsylvania.

Passengers could transfer from the Western Maryland Railway train to the Thurmont Trolley in Thurmont, MD. Photo courtesy of the Western Maryland Railway Historical Society.

Charles E. Cassell, editor of the Catoctin Clarion, suggested the name Thurmont. It is a combination of two words from two different languages. Thur is from the German word for "gateway," and Mont is from the French word for "mountain." Cassell said Thurmont meant "Gateway to the Mountains," and West Main Street in the town leads up Catoctin Mountain, so the name was appropriate.

However, it was not an immediate hit among the townspeople. It took multiple community votes to reach the consensus to make the name change.

Once the residents had decided on a new name, it took an act by the Maryland General Assembly to formally change the name of Mechanicstown to Thurmont on January 18, 1894.

So, the Thurmont's name was changed, in part, to avoid confusion at the Western Maryland Railroad train stations.

184

Playing a Game of "Ride" and Seek

Lester Albright, Leonard Bowling and Wilson Shulte scattered as one of their friends covered his eyes and began counting. They scurried around, searching for a place to hide; someplace they wouldn't be found. Crossing into the freight yards for the Western Maryland Railroad in Gettysburg, the boys climbed into a box car Friday morning, November 21, 1929.

Their hiding spot worked better than expected because they weren't found until Sunday afternoon.

As the boys hid quietly in the box car, a trainman walked by making one last inspection of the train cars. Seeing the open box car, he shut the door and locked it.

Surprised, it took the boys a few moments before they realized they had been locked inside. When they did, they jumped from their hiding places and began banging on the door trying to attract attention. Then the train began moving!

Thus began their 118-mile journey to Cumberland, Md.

Fighting down their initial panic, the boys thought it would be an adventure to take a short ride on the train, but then minutes turned into hours and the hours into days. The train did make one stop in Highfield, Pa., so that the train could be shifted to the main line of the Western Maryland Railroad.

The Western Maryland Railway began as the Baltimore, Carroll and Frederick Rail Road in 1852. It started in Baltimore and was built westward, eventually reaching Hagerstown, Md., in 1872. Within a year after its founding, the company became the Western Maryland Rail Road Company and then later still, the Western Maryland Railway Company.

The company built an extension into Pennsylvania in 1881 and connected to the Harrisburg and Potomac Rail Road in 1886. Next, the Western Maryland Rail Road connected to the Baltimore and Ohio Railroad at Cherry Run, W. Va., in 1892. This connection improved freight traffic on the railroad.

An extension that ran to Cumberland was completed in 1906. From there, the railroad would extend to Connellsville, Pa., and south into West Virginia.

"The first gnawing of hunger over-took the lads Friday evening. It was too cold in the car to sleep either night, and the boys kept awake by moving around," reported the *Gettysburg Star and Sentinel* on November 29, 1929.

The western portal of the Stickpile Tunnel in Allegany County along the Western Maryland Railway. Photo courtesy of Wikimedia Commons.

On Sunday morning, a surprised trainman unlocked and opened the box car in the Western Maryland train yards in Ridgeley, W. Va. The boys jumped out and asked how to get back to Gettysburg. The trainman turned the boys over to a railroad detective named Hanson. He listened to their story and turned them over to the Salvation Army in Cumberland and notified a detective there named Charles Wilson.

"After eating some hot food and a sleep, the trio were none the worse for their experience," the *Star and Sentinel* reported.

Wilson notified the boys' parents and Levi Albright and John Bowling, fathers of two of the boys, drove to Cumberland to pick up the boys on Sunday afternoon and drive them home.

The families had notified the Pennsylvania State Police when their sons hadn't returned home from playing on Friday, but the police hadn't been able to find any hint as to the boys' whereabouts.

As passenger service declined in the 1950's, the Western Maryland discontinued it altogether in 1959. By 1973, the Western Maryland Railway became part of the Chessie System, which in turn became CSX Transportation in 1987.

What's In a Name?

Officially, the Western Maryland Railway had two names. Pre-20th century, it was called the Western Maryland Railroad. Post-20th century, it became the Western Maryland Railway. This is because the Western Maryland Railroad was sold in 1902 and reorganized as the Western Maryland Railway. This was the beginning of the Fuller Syndicate's involvement with the railroad as George Gould sought to create a transcontinental railroad system.

Although this is the official reason for the name change, unofficially, it was done to give the railroad a name that suggested it was modern. At this time in history, some railroads changed the word "railroad" in their names to "railway." It made no difference in a legal sense, but it was believed that projected a sense of modernity. Also, the Western Maryland Railroad directors felt it gave the railroad a fresh start after its financial difficulties.

However, the railroad also had more than its fair share of nicknames.

A popular nickname for the railroad was "Wild Mary." It used the railroad's initials, WM, but it also referred to the often scenic and rugged routes of the railroad. Trent Carbaugh described one section of the Western Maryland Railway as "neither easy nor safe areas, combining steep slippery hills, wetlands/swamps, open wells around old farmsteads, and the ever present acres of multi-flora rose."

Similarly, some railfans called the Western Maryland Railway "The Road of the Scenic Route" because of the beautiful views along the routes. American-Rails.com says, "While aspects of the system posed operational difficulties (notably Black Fork Grade), the WM offered some of the most fantastic photographic opportunities one could ever hope for as it navigated through the Appalachians of central/eastern West Virginia, parts of Maryland, and southwestern Pennsylvania."

Some people used a similar nickname, "The Wild Mary Line," which is you say it fast enough or with an accent, can also sound like "The Western Maryland."

The railroad was also called "The Alphabet Route." This came from the fact that the Western Maryland Railway was made up of 29 smaller railroads. Many of these railroad typically went by their initials, such as W&LE (Wheeling and Lake Erie), P&WV (Pittsburgh and West Virginia Railway), RDG (Reading Railroad). When you start putting all those abbreviations together on a map, it begins looking more like a Scrabble board than a railroad map.

The Western Maryland Railway was also called "The Fast Freight Line." This was actually the railroad's official slogan that focused on its speed and efficiency in hauling freight from the Appalachian Mountains to the Chesapeake Bay. It was used often enough to also become a nickname.

While "The Fast Freight Line" was used to attract business customers, "The Lord Baltimore Line" was used to promote passenger service on the Western Maryland Railroad. It gave the railroad an air of elegance and tied into the company's heritage.

Whichever nickname was used, it was used with affection. The choice depended on what the person using it liked about the railroad whether it was the views, the fast freight service, or the elegant passenger service.

A train waiting at the Western Maryland Railway station in Cumberland, MD. Photo courtesy of Western Maryland's Historical Library.

Acknowledgements

I wanted to thank all of those people who helped me put the *Secrets of the Western Maryland Railway* together. The longer I work as a writer, the more I realize that while one person may publish a book, the effort is much richer when others assist.

I've been writing articles about the history of this region for nearly two decades. I've been doing the Secrets books for nine years, and the series is very popular. *Secrets of Garrett County* was the first book in the series. I wrote it way back in 2017, and I have a list of potential topics for future Secrets books that I will never be able to complete. *Secrets of the Western Maryland Railway* is No. 10.

One great local resource for finding the stories in this book was digitized editions of the county newspapers found on various websites. I was also helped by members of the Western Maryland Railway Historical Society in Union Bridge, Md. They shared their knowledge and resources to help me along.

Since many of the stories in the Secrets books have appeared in newspapers and magazines, I get e-mails and phone calls from readers with new ideas and additional information that I try to incorporate into these book versions of the stories.

Finally, I'd like to thank Grace Eyler with E Plus in Emmitsburg, Md., for not only creating another great-looking cover but also being able to create the template for the Secrets series.

I have probably missed someone who I'll remember after this book goes to print. If so, it's not because I didn't appreciate your input. I sometimes get confused juggling all the projects that I do. If I did leave you out, mention it to me.

Meanwhile, I'm off to work on my next project.

James Rada, Jr.
December 27, 2025

About the Author

James Rada, Jr. is an Amazon.com bestselling author of historical fiction and non-fiction history. They include the popular books *Strike the Fuse, Canawlers,* and *Battlefield Angels: The Daughters of Charity Work as Civil War Nurses.*

He lives in Gettysburg, Pa., where he works as a freelance writer. James has received numerous awards from the Maryland-Delaware-DC Press Association, Associated Press, Maryland State Teachers Association, Society of Professional Journalists, and Community Newspaper Holdings, Inc. for his newspaper writing.

If you would like to be kept up to date on new books being published by James or ask him questions, he can be reached by e-mail at *jimrada@yahoo.com.*

To see James' other books or to order copies on-line, go to *www.jamesrada.com.*

PLEASE LEAVE A REVIEW

If you enjoyed this book, please help other readers find it. Reviews help authors get more exposure for their books. Please take a few minutes to review this book at *Goodreads.com.* Thank you, and if you sign up for his mailing list at *jamesrada.com*, you can get FREE ebooks.

WANT TO KNOW MORE SECRETS?

Find out the little-known stories and hidden history of Maryland and Pennsylvania with the Secrets series from James Rada, Jr.

Available wherever books are sold.

www.ingramcontent.com/pod-product-compliance
Lightning Source LLC
Chambersburg PA
CBHW051526150726
47997CB00001B/400